Pitfalls in Genealogical Research

By Milton Rubincam

Ancestry®

Library of Congress Catalog Card Number 87-70105
ISBN 0-916489-28-0

Copyright 1987
Ancestry Incorporated
P.O. Box 476
Salt Lake City, Utah 84110
All rights reserved

First printing 1987
10 9 8 7 6

Printed in the United States of America

CONTENTS

PREFACE

On 16 November 1954 I delivered a talk on "Pitfalls in Genealogical Research" before the Fort McHenry Chapter of the Daughters of the American Revolution (DAR). I repeated it on 23 November 1954 before the Columbia Chapter, DAR, and on 8 January 1955 before the National Genealogical Society. It was published in the *National Genealogical Society Quarterly* for June 1955, and reprinted in Noel C. Stevenson's *The Genealogical Reader* in 1958. Since then, I have given scores of talks on the same subject before many societies and institutes, adding to or changing the material as circumstances warranted. Taped versions have appeared in *The Connecticut Nutmegger* and other magazines and journals.

This monograph is an extension of those lectures. It is based in part on my own experiences and in great measure on a wide range of reading. It is designed to help the beginning genealogist avoid the pitfalls into which we all have fallen—and some of us still do, if we are not careful. Elizabeth L. Nichols, in one of her small basic books on genealogical research, devotes a whole page to a single word printed in large letters: "THINK!" It is sound advice for all genealogists, amateur, avocational, or professional.

CHAPTER 1

THE SANCTITY OF THE PRINTED WORD

The late Dr. Jean Stephenson, director of the Institute of Genealogical Research,[1] used to begin her lectures with: "I don't believe a thing I see in print!" This declaration always shook-up the beginning genealogists in her class, for they had accepted printed genealogies as gospel. But the sad fact is that many genealogies and family histories contain erroneous statements because the compiler has accepted the unverified statements of previously published works, has failed to go to the original sources for information, and has not evaluated the evidence. In many cases, errors have been repeated in book after book for a period of years, because the compilers made no attempt to prove or disprove them.

A classic case in point is the Smalley–FitzRandolph pedigree. O. B. Leonard, a well-known New Jersey genealogist at the turn of the century, published three articles on the Smalley and FitzRandolph families of Piscataway Township, Middlesex County, New Jersey. (See the 17 October 1902 issue of *The Daily Press*, of Plainfield, N.J.; *Proceedings of the New Jersey Historical Society*, 3rd series, vol. 5 (1908), pp. 160 *et seq*, which is for no apparent reason reprinted in *Proceedings*, New Series, vol. 5 (1920), pp. 35 *et seq*.) According to Mr. Leonard, a certain Jonathan Smalley, born 10 April 1683, married *ca.* 1707, Sarah Fitz-Randolph, the eldest child of John and Sarah FitzRandolph. It is a matter of record that in the course of three centuries more than a dozen Smalley–FitzRandolph marriages have occurred. Consequently, Jonathan's marriage to Sarah FitzRandolph seemed to be a valid union. Mr. Leonard's 1920 *Proceedings* article was picked up and reprinted in Dr.

Orra Eugene Monnette's *First Settlers of Ye Plantations of Piscataway and Woodbridge, Olde East New Jersey, 1664-1714*, Part 3 (1931), pp. 435 *et seq.*[2] Other works that carried the Jonathan-Sarah claim were Lewis V. F. Randolph's *Fitz-Randolph Traditions: A Story of a Thousand Years* (1907); Dr. John E. Stillwell's *Historical and Genealogical Miscellaney: Data Relating to the Settlement and Settlers of New York and New Jersey*, vol. 3, p. 793; Francis Bazley Lee's *Genealogical and Memorial History of the State of New Jersey* (1910), vol. 3, p. 763; and the *Mayflower Index.*

The principal value of Sarah FitzRandolph's ancestry to Jonathan Smalley's descendants was because she was a great-granddaughter of Samuel Fuller, and great-great-granddaughter of Edward Fuller, both of whom had come to America aboard the *Mayflower* in 1620. This provided an opportunity for Jonathan Smalley's posterity to join the Mayflower Society, which is what many did.[3]

Meanwhile, the Smalley-FitzRandolph marriage was undergoing a critical review. In the July 1939 issue of the *Genealogical Magazine of New Jersey*, a very competent Philadelphia genealogist, Lewis D. Cook, published an article entitled "Coriell-Smalley Bible Records." The Bible, printed in 1818 by E. & J. White for The American Bible Society, was originally owned by David Smalley (1766-1854), of Bernards Township, Somerset County, New Jersey. In the family record, David wrote that his grandfather, Jonathan Smalley, was "marrid (*sic*) to Sarah Bird..." Earlier, in 1934, Lora A. W. Underhill, in her *Genealogy of Edward Small*, wrote (p. 32): "It has been frequently asserted that Jonathan[3] Smalley married Sarah Fitz Randolph. No record of such a marriage has been found, while it is definitely recorded in the Coriell-Smalley Bible that Jonathan Smalley married Sarah Bird, as stated above. The margin of the Bible page is torn or worn, so that, possibly, the name may have had another syllable. The name of Birdsall is common in the region, while that of Bird is rare."

In 1950 Louise Aymar Christian and Howard Stelle Fitz Randolph published *The Descendants of Edward Fitz Randolph and Elizabeth Blossom, 1630-1950.* They treat the claim with proper caution: "SARAH[3] b. April 25, 1682; often said to have married JONATHAN SMALLEY, but an old Bible record shows he married Sarah Bird."

In spite of the warning put forth by these writers, descendants of Jonathan Smalley continued to join the Mayflower Society through Sarah FitzRandolph. Some years ago the Society established its Five Generation Project. It was determined to reinvestigate all of the *Mayflower* families, and to publish the results in a series of volumes. All traditions, unauthenticated statements, fairy tales, and fictions that had abounded through the centuries were to be thrown out. Only documentary evidence establishing the genealogical relationships could be allowed. For each questionable pedigree, three referees were chosen to consider the problem and to make recommendations. For the Smalley–FitzRandolph project the referees were Dr. Gilbert H. Doane, author of the classic *Searching for Your Ancestors*; Dr. Kenneth Richards, archivist of the state of New Jersey; and myself. (None of us knew who the others were until after we had rendered our reports and the Society had reached a decision.) We studied photocopies of the evidence, both pro and con, and all recommended that the Smalley–FitzRandolph line should be dropped from the list of eligible ancestors of the Society. We felt that David Smalley, who made precise records of his family in the Bible, knew who his grandmother was, and that her name was Sarah Bird (Birdsall ?) and not Sarah FitzRandolph.

What led O. B. Leonard to declare that Jonathan Smalley had married Sarah FitzRandolph? The evidence is in the O. B. Leonard papers in the New Jersey Historical Society at Newark. On a later visit to do research at the Historical Society, I examined the Smalley and FitzRandolph files in his collection.

The problem began with Mrs. Ashbel Welch (*nee* Emma Finney), of Germantown, Philadelphia, Pennsylvania, who provided Leonard with data about the Smalley family. On 6 October 1902 she wrote a long letter to the genealogist about the Smalleys' and FitzRandolphs', both of which were among the founding families of the Seventh Day Baptist Church of Piscataway at New Market, Middlesex County, New Jersey. Her researchers could not find the name of the wife of her ancestor Jonathan Smalley. A list of six Sarahs living at that time was sent to her; the marriages of all could be accounted for in the church records except a certain Sarah FitzRandolph for whom no husband was found. As a matter of fact, the Sarah FitzRandolph mentioned in the church records was a member of the family by marriage; she was Sarah Molleson, who in 1712 became the wife of David FitzRandolph (1690/91-1773), a first cousin of the alleged wife of Jonathan Smalley.[4]

Among the persons to whom Leonard applied for genealogical data was William L. Smalley, Sr., of Plainfield, New Jersey. William Smalley provided Leonard with a newspaper clipping from *The Daily Press* of 18 June 1889, which clearly stated that Jonathan Smalley married Sarah Bird. Leonard ignored this, and published his article asserting that Jonathan married Sarah FitzRandolph, daughter of John and Sarah. However, Mrs. Welch continued her investigations, caught up with the family Bible, and sent a photocopy of the family record to Mr. Leonard (5 July 1904). In spite of this, Leonard made no retraction of his erroneous statement and repeated it in the 1908 and 1920 issues of the New Jersey Historical Society's *Proceedings*. He thus laid the groundwork for the descendants of Jonathan and Sarah (Bird/Birdsall) Smalley to be mistakenly admitted to the Mayflower Society.

Reproduction of a Page From David Smalley's Family Bible. It
Shows (at top of page) That His Grandfather, Jonathan Smalley,
Married Sarah Bird—Not Sarah FitzRandolph

This is not an isolated case. The same story about other families could be repeated hundreds of times. The moral of the story is: one must not accept statements merely because they appear in print. Every link in the genealogical chain must be verified by documentary evidence.

Notes

1. During her administration, the Institute was conducted by the National Archives and American University, Washington, D.C., under the sponsorship of the American Society of Genealogists. In the 1970s the American University withdrew from the program and the National Archives continued to operate it alone as the National Institute of Genealogical Research, until 1982 when it relinquished control for budgetary reasons. Since then it has been administered by the Genealogical Coordinating Committee, composed of the presidents of a number of genealogical organizations.

2. Students of New Jersey genealogy are aware that Mr. Monnette's work must be used with caution. Many of his statements are unverified and have been found to be in error. He assembled a vast amount of information which may be used as clues for providing further research but must not be considered as Holy Writ.

3. The FitzRandolphs of New Jersey belonged to what is probably the only American family that can be traced in the male line for a thousand years. They are descended from the FitzRandalls of Spennithorne and Middleham Castle in Yorkshire, and the latter are sprung through many generations from Geoffrey, Duke of Brittany from 992 until his death in 1008. There are two generations in this long pedigree that need strengthening, but the evidence is clear that they are of the same family. (See *Edward FitzRandolph Branch Lines, Allied Families, and English and Norman Ancestry. A Family Genealogy, 860-1975*, pp. 579-89; Norman and English ancestry traced by Sir Anthony Wagner, K.C.V.O., Garter Principal King of Arms, The College of Arms, London. See also John Insley Coddington, "Bigod Pedigree," in Adams and Weis, *The Magna Charta Sureties, 1215*, 3rd rev. ed., edited by Walter Lee Sheppard, Jr., 1979, pp. 110-12.

4. Louise Aymar Christian and Howard Stelle Fitz Randolph, *The Descendants of Edward Fitz Randolph and Elizabeth Blossom, 1630-1950*. Grateful acknowledgement is made to the late Miss Lucy Mary Kellogg, then chairman of the Five Generation Project of the Mayflower Society, for permission to use the Smalley–FitzRandolph case in speeches and articles; also to Stuart P. Lloyd, historian of the New Jer-

sey Society of Mayflower Descendants, and B. C. McGunnigle, East Greenwich, Rhode Island, for additional material on the problem.

CHAPTER 2

RELATIONSHIPS OF SIMILAR OR IDENTICAL SURNAMES

O ne of our great failings when we first undertake to trace our ancestry is to assume a connection with a family of similar or identical surname. This is an especially dangerous procedure, for until we develop the ability to analyze the evidence at our disposal and to deduce conclusions, based on the preponderance of the evidence, we find ourselves annexing ancestors who do not belong to us.

Many examples come readily to mind. An Indiana family claimed that their ancestor, William Moffett, married Isabella, daughter of John and Gertrude (Thompson) Read, and granddaughter of George Read of Delaware, a signer of the Declaration of Independence. Several descendants of William Moffett became members, in good faith, of the National Society Daughters of the American Revolution.[1]

This allegation is not supported by Major Harmon Pumpelly Read's valuable and well-documented *Rossiana* (1908), containing detailed accounts of the Ross and Read families. On page 270 he shows that the signer's son, John Read (1769-1854), married Martha Meredith (not Gertrude Thompson), and had five children: John Meredith, Edward, Henry Meredith, Margaret Meredith (died in infancy), and another Margaret Meredith (unmarried). The "daughter" Isabella is conspicuous by reason of her absence. Further research discloses that the Isabella Read who married William Moffett belonged to a relatively obscure family of Reed of Washington County, Virginia.[2] Obviously, the Indiana descendants of William and Isabella (Read) Moffett had assumed a connection with the great Delaware family because of the similarity of name, and, perhaps, because of the signer's fame.

Another case of mistaken identity involved families named Tuttle and Tuthill. It was said that Samuel Tuttle, of Hanover, Morris County, New Jersey, who died in 1762, married in 1751 Rachel, daughter of Col. Jacob Ford, Sr., and sister of Col. Jacob Ford, Jr., whose mansion at Morristown was General Washington's headquarters during one phase of the American Revolution.[3] Another work asserted that Samuel's wife was not Rachel Ford but Sarah, daughter of the senior Colonel Ford. Moreover, the work spelled the name Tuthill, and stated that he died in 1814, fifty-two years after 1762.[4] As the Tuttles are in my wife's ancestry, I tackled this problem and learned the following: (1) Samuel Tuttle, who died in 1762, married in 1751 Rachel Gould (not Ford); (2) Samuel Tuthill, who died in 1814, was a prominent man in Morris County affairs and married Sarah Ford; (3) the two Samuels were born within a short time of each other (Tuthill, ca. 1723, Tuttle, 1724); (4) they lived in the same neighborhood; and (5) Moses, brother of Samuel Tuttle, married Jane Ford, and so became a brother-in-law of Samuel Tuthill.[5]

Additional cases of assuming relationship to families of similar or identical surnames will be discussed later in this monograph.

Notes

1. DAR Lineage Books, 58:258-59 (1906), 79:202 (1910), and 81:256 (1910).

2. This information is based upon family papers from the late Mrs. Isabel Paflin, of Tenafly, New Jersey. When I visited her in the 1940s, she was too ill to see me, but her papers were made available to me by her daughter, Mrs. Roberta Petty. The latter's daughter, Miss Isobel Petty, at a much later date kindly lent me a family album which provided genealogical data about the Reed and Moffett families. I confirmed the connection by researching court records in the Archives Division of the Virginia State Library.

3. Information contained in: George Frederick Tuttle, *The Descendants of William and Elizabeth Tuttle* (1883), p. 319. Others who repeated his claim that Samuel Tuttle married Rachel Ford were William Ogden Wheeler, compiler; Lawrence Van Alstine; and the Reverend Charles Burr Ogden, Ph.D.; editors, *The Ogden Family in America. Elizabethtown Branch* (1907) p. 64, and Francis Bazley Lee, *Genealogical and Memorial History of the State of New Jersey* (1910), 1:166.

4. Miss Elizabeth M. Bamford, "Ford Family Notes," *New York Genealogical and Biographical Record*, April 1922, pp. 166-67.

5. Milton Rubincam, "The Identity of the Wife of Samuel Tuttle, of Hanover, Morris County, New Jersey," *Genealogical Magazine of New Jersey*, April 1939, pp. 38-42. To this article the late Charles Carroll Gardner, then associate editor of the magazine, added an addendum quoting the family history of Samuel Tuthill as given by W. H. Tuthill in a letter preserved in the Yale University Library.

CHAPTER 3

FAMILY TRADITION

Donald Lines Jacobus, for many years dean of American genealogists until his death in 1970, once wrote: "Tradition is a chronic deceiver, and those who put faith in it are self-deceivers. This is not to say that tradition is invariably false. Sometimes a modicum of fact increases in geometric ratio as the lineage claimed increases in grandeur."[1]

After citing the popular traditions of the Rogers's families, claiming descent from John Rogers (the English martyr of the sixteenth century) and Adams's families fondly believing they are related to the second and sixth presidents of the United States, Jacobus went on to discuss two traditions in his own family, alleged descents from John Wilmot, second Earl of Rochester (1647-1680), and from a seventeenth century settler in New Amsterdam, Anneke Jans. The last-named lady is an extremely popular traditional ancestress, because her descendants like to think that through her they can inherit $850,000,000 worth of real estate in New York City now occupied by Trinity Church. They also like to think that through her they are sprung from William the Silent, Prince of Orange (1533-1584), the founder of the Dutch Republic. Both of these delusions have been exploded, but even so, some of Anneke Jans's descendants still live in their fantasy world.[2]

My own family had a beautiful tradition. As Americans, we often feel that there is something romantic about a Huguenot line of descent. My uncle, Albert Rubincam, who introduced me to genealogy when I was ten years old, related that we were of Huguenot origin. Our name was originally Rubinchamp, meaning "red field" or "field of blood," a battlefield on which our forefathers nobly shed their blood for the Catholic kings who persecuted them. (The logic of this I never quite understood.) In the dreadful Massacre of St. Bartholomew's Day (24 August 1572) we were all but wiped out. That did it, so far as we were concerned. What was left of us split into two branches, mine going to Germany and the other to Wales.[3] My uncle had this story from my grandfather, who probably had heard it from earlier generations.

This tradition is far too detailed to be believable. When I became proficient in genealogical research, could read French and German, and had caused professional researches to be conducted in our part of Germany (Hessen), I learned the true facts. Instead of being French, we were German. Instead of being valiant soldiers of the king of France we were pious clergymen in the Landgraviate of Hessen-Kassel (of the Reformed, or Calvinist Church). And instead of our name being Rubinchamp, mistranslated as "red field," it was Rubekamp (Rubenkamp), signifying "turnip field."[4]

The Huguenot tradition is a popular one among Americans. Any name that sounds even remotely French is proclaimed as Huguenot. I have read of a Brown family that claimed to be originally French Le-Brun, although the immigrant ancestor was clearly English. I have heard of a family bearing the fine old English name of Pemberton claiming its French origin. It must be remembered that from the Norman Conquest (1066) French families have filtered into England. In the Middle Ages some of our Plantagenet kings married French princesses, and many French families followed them into the island. The persecutions in France in the sixteenth century also brought many French families to England. In April 1598 King Henry IV of France and Navarre—who was formerly a Huguenot but turned Catholic when he succeeded to the throne with the laconic comment, "Paris is worth a mass"—issued the Edict of Nantes whereby his Protestant subjects were granted a large measure of religious freedom and full civil rights. Under his successors the Huguenots did not fare so well, and persecutions began again. His grandson, Louis XIV, revoked the Edict of Nantes on 18 October 1685 and the Huguenots were subjected to a merciless onslaught of persecution. They fled to Protestant countries that were friendly to them: England, Switzerland,[5] Hessen-Kassel, Brandenburg-Prussia, and the Netherlands. Thousands of them came to America, but this presents another pitfall. The Huguenots that lived in Germany generally became Germans, taking German names and speaking German. When they settled in Pennsylvania, it was difficult to distinguish them from their Germanic neighbors, and great care must be exercised in tracing them. For a detailed account with bibliographies, see Cameron Allen, "Huguenot Migrations," in the American Society of Genealogists's *Genealogical Research: Methods and Sources*, Kenn Stryker-Rodda, ed., (1983):308-40.[6]

Another favorite tradition is that of the "Three Brothers." It is amazing how many families were founded by three brothers! They had no parents, no homes abroad; presumably they floated down from heaven and landed in one of the colonies. This tradition often originated because three men of the same surname were found in the same community at the same time, and a rash assumption was made that they were brothers. Only by methodical research through court records and, if they exist, family papers can such a relationship be sustained. Some families were indeed founded by three brothers. I am descended from Peter Wright, who with his brothers Anthony and Nicholas and others co-founded Oyster Bay, Long Island, New York, in 1653. Their relationship was proved by documentary evidence. In their case we do have an ancient memorandum showing that they had parents and grandparents living in Norfolk County, England. Some years ago John Frederick Dorman published serially, in his magazine *The Virginia Genealogist*, a genealogy of the Chilton family of Lancaster, Northampton, and Westmoreland counties, Virginia, founded in the 1660s by the brothers (so proved by documentary evidence) Stephen, George, and John Chilton. In their case, the English ancestry is uncertain. There are probably other families founded by two, three, or four brothers, with perhaps a sister or two thrown in for good measure. But such a relationship must be established by incontrovertible evidence, not by assumption on the part of the researcher.

Just as the Huguenot tradition is popular among us, so is the tradition of descent from a Hessian soldier who was brought to this country during the Revolutionary War to fight for King George III and became so imbued with democratic principles that he deserted from the Anglo-Hessian forces and founded a stalwart American family. Many years ago a woman told me a fantastic story about her ancestor who, she said, was a son of Emperor Joseph II's prime minister. The youth ran away from home, joined the Hessian forces, deserted to the Continental Army and, because of his remarkable military ability, was appointed a captain on George Washington's staff, and was present when the Commander-in-Chief delivered his "Farewell Address" to his officers. I cannot now remember the man's name, but I recall searching the military records in the National Archives and Heitman's *Historical Register of Officers in the Continental Army* without finding a trace of him. As I found him in the 1790 census of Luzerne County, Pennsylvania, I suggested she would do well to begin her search in the Luzerne County courthouse. I also pointed out that her ancestor could not have been a son of Joseph II's "prime minister" (who actually bore the title of chancellor) because this official had an entirely different surname. I'm afraid the lady was unconvinced, for she replied most indignantly, reaffirming the truth of her story. As I've lost the ancestor's name, I am unable to check the computerized indices to the Hessian troops that have since been published to ascertain if he actually served with these forces.

We must clarify the term "Hessian," which is often used incorrectly. Six states of the old Holy Roman Empire allied themselves with Great Britain in the effort to crush the rebellious colonists, namely: Hessen-Kassel, Hessen-Hanau, Ansbach-Bayreuth, Brunswick (Braunschweig), Anhalt, and Waldeck. The greater proportion of the soldiers were in the forces of Hessen-Kassel and Hessen-Hanau, hence we popularly (but incorrectly) refer to all of Britain's German auxiliary troops as "Hessians."

Many an American family with a German name has assumed that its first ancestor in this country was a "Hessian" soldier who deserted, married a native girl, and had children. Those who boast of such a descent almost always claim that their progenitor was an officer—the German troops seemingly had no noncommissioned officers or privates! The article on General George A. Custer in *The Dictionary of American Biography* alleges he was descended from a "Hessian officer," but it is more likely he was descended from Paulus Kuster, an early settler of Germantown, Pennsylvania. A claim was made at one time that the Baumgardner family of Lancaster County, Pennsylvania, was derived from a Hessian soldier, but members of that family were in that colony by 1729.

There are documented cases of such a line of descent. The late Dr. Arthur Adams, first president of the American Society of Genealogists, had an ancestor named Oswald Gutberlet, who was born 18 November 1756 at Unterweissenborn, Hessen-Kassel. The baptismal record of Oswald Schott (from the parish register of Schenklengsfled, in which Unterweissenborn was located) stated on 8 November 1776, that the child's godfather was Oswald Gutberlet, "a soldier in the Prince Carl Regiment, in America."[7]

There is now a way to prove whether an ancestor was a Hessian soldier in the Revolutionary War. From 1972 to 1976 the Archivschule Marburg, Institut Archivweissenschaft at Marburg, Hessen, West Germany, published five volumes of computerized indices of soldiers who served in America from 1776 to 1783. The first four volumes deal with men who were in Hessian military units; the fifth volume lists men in the Waldeck Regiment. The title of the work is: *Hessische Truppen im amerikanischen Unabhangigkeitskrieg (HETRINA)*. The introduction, in German, is followed by a summary in English explaining how to read the military records. Taking Dr. Adams's ancestor as an example, we learn (Band II, nos. 4561-4562) that Oswald Gutberlet was born at Unterweissenborn in 1755/56 (the birth years are based on ages at time of recruitment). He was a Gemeiner (private) in the Fifth Company of the Prince Carl Regiment, and he deserted in May 1783.

Dr. Erhardt Stadtler's work, published at Nurnberg, Bavaria, in 1956, *Die Ansbach-Bayreuther Truppen im amerikanischen Unabhangig-*

4551	GUNDLACH	NIKOLAUS	1727/28	PFERDSDORF	X6221♦	GE	LOB2	01	5.1783	SR205
4552	GUNDLACH	WILHELM	0/0	ERSRODE	D6431♦	GE	MIR2	09	4.1780	8819/6
4553	GUNDLACH	WILHELM	1754/55	ERSRODE	D6431♦	GE	MIR2	01	3.1783	SR513
4554	GUNDLACH		1756/57	MELSUNGEN	D3508♦	GE	MIR5	01	4.1775	SR512
4555	GUNDLACH		1756/57	MELSUNGEN	D3508♦	KR	MIR5	19	3.1783	SR513
4556	GUNKLER		0/0	MELSUNGEN	D3508♦	GE	MIR5	01	5.1784	8819/38
4557	GUTBERLET	JAKOB	1751/52	NIEDERAULA	D6434♦	GE	CAR1	01	0.1783	SR471
4558	GUTBERLET	JOHANNES	1743/44	SCHENKLENGSFELD	D6431♦	GE	CAR1	01	4.1775	SR470
4559	GUTBERLET	JOHANNES	1742/43	SCHENKLENGSFELD	D6431♦	GE	CAR1	01	0.1783	SR471
4560	GUTBERLET	LUDWIG	1753/54	HERSFELD/HIRSCHF.	D6430♦	GE	LOB1	01	6.1783	SR205
4561	GUTBERLET	OSWALD	1755/56	UNTERWEISENBORN	D6431♦	GE	CAR5	12	5.1783	8824/13
4562	GUTBERLET	OSWALD	1755/56	UNTERWEISENBORN	D6431♦	GE	CAR5	01	0.1783	SR471
4563	GUTHARD	DANIEL	1749/50	BORKEN	D3587♦	GE	DON4	01	0.1775	SR387
4564	GUTHARD	DANIEL	0/0	BORKEN	D3587♦	KR	DON4	04	4.1780	8841/33
4565	GUTHARD	DANIEL	1749/50	BORKEN	D3587♦	KR	DON4	01	0.1783	SR388
4566	GUTHARD/GOTHARD	DANIEL	0/0	BORKEN	D3587♦	GE	DON4	12	3.1784	8841/133
4567	GUTHARD	DAVID	1764/65	GENSUNGEN	D3582♦	GE	DON4	02	2.1779	8841/19
4568	GUTHARD	DAVID	1756/57	GENSUNGEN	D3582♦	GE	DON4	12	10.1782	8841/98
4569	GUTHARD	GEORG	1741/42	DORCHHEIM	D6251	GE	DON3	01	0.1783	SR388
4570	GUTHARD	HENRICH		VERNA	D3579♦	GE	BOS2	12	5.1783	8826/2
4571	GUTHARD	JOHANNES	1755/56	DICKERSHAUSEN	D3589♦	GE	DON5	20	0.1775	SR387
4572	GUTHARD	JOHANNES	1755/56	DICKERSHAUSEN	D3589♦	GE	DON5	12	1.1783	8841/127
4573	GUTHARD	JOHANNES	1755/56	DICKERSHAUSEN	D3589♦	GE	DON5	01	0.1783	SR388
4574	GUTHE	JOHANNES	1751/52	MOLLRODE	D3501♦	GE	MIR3	01	3.1783	SR513
4575	GUTHEIL	JOHANNES	1754/55	MARDORF	D3589♦	GE	DON5	20	0.1775	SR387
4576	GUTHEIL	JOHANNES	1754/55	MARDORF	D3589♦	GE	DON5	01	0.1783	SR388
4577	GUTHMANN	GEORG	1751/52	GREBENSTEIN	D3523♦	GE	BOS2	01	0.1783	SR484
4578	GUTHMANN	GEORG	1751/52	GREBENSTEIN	D3523♦	GE	BOS2	07	8.1777	8826/18
4579	GUTBERLET	LUDWIG	0/0	HERSFELD/HIRSCHF.	D6430♦	GE	LOB1	02	9.1781	72,3,3,34
4580	HAACK	CHRISTOPH	0/0			GE	LOB2	07	4.1776	4H412/265

This Page From the _Hessische Truppen im amerikanischen Unabhangigkeitskrieg_ Shows the Military Record of Oswald Gutberlet, an Ancestor of the Good Bartlett Family of New Jersey

keitskrieg, 1777-1783, is entirely in German but, with a good German dictionary at hand, even the researcher who knows little or no German can gain facts about the men recorded therein.

Further aids to researching ancestors who possibly served with the German mercenary troops are the *German-American Genealogical Research Monographs* compiled and published by Clifford Neal Smith. He has identified many soldiers of the Hessian, Brunswicker, and Ansbach-Bayreuther troops who deserted.

The books cited above may be found in most of the large libraries in the United States.

The Johannes Schwalm Historical Association of Lyndhurst, Ohio, devotes itself to researching, collecting, and publishing (in its annual journal) information on the descendants of Hessian soldiers.[8]

There are many other traditions that could be cited. Very often the tradition that a family is heir to great wealth results in fly-by-night organizations springing up to make a claim for it. Often such outfits are fraudulent affairs, such as the Anneke Jans association that Mr. Jacobus's father joined in an honest (but mistaken) belief that he was the lady's descendant. In Delaware, one prominent early settler was Carl Christoffersson Springer. His descendants were led to believe they were heirs to vast tracts of land in Wilmington. Early in this century a "Springer Heirs Corporation 1913, U.S. American and Canada" was founded but nothing further was heard of it.

There is, of course, the age-old tradition of a family being heir to an ancient title. Many English and American families named Hall have traditionally claimed descent from William Shakespeare through his elder daughter Susanna, wife of Dr. John Hall. The fact remains, however, that the Bard of Stratford-on-Avon does not have a single descendant living today. The last member of his direct line was his granddaughter, Elizabeth Hall, wife of Sir John Barnard (Bernard), who was buried on 17 February 1669/70.[9]

Our quotation from Jacobus at the beginning of this chapter noted that some traditions have a "modicum of fact." Two such cases come readily to mind. We will simply summarize these cases here; the evidence has been published in detail elsewhere.

In the 1690s a German physician and surgeon, Dr. Johannes Richter von Kroninschildt, after serving at sea as a ship's doctor, settled in Boston, where he died in 1711. By his wife, Elizabeth Allen, he had five children, of whom two sons settled in Salem, Massachusetts, where they founded the prominent family of Crowninshield, the anglicized version of the name. There had long been a tradition in the family that the doctor was a graduate of the University of Leipzig, in Saxony, from which he had been expelled for participating in a duel. One of his descendants, G. Andrews Moriarty, a noted authority on English medieval genealogy, decided to test the tradition. The researches he commissioned found that Dr. von Kroninschildt was baptized in the Church of St. Thomas at Leipzig on 22 June 1661, the illegitimate son of Caspar Richter of Halle, a student at the University of Leipzig, by a girl named Maria Hahn. It was believed by the German researchers that Caspar was expelled from the university because of this liaison. He must have been of good family because when he later married another girl he was described as "the noble, strong, and valiant gentleman, Johann Caspar Richter of Dresden," where he later lived. So the modicum of truth is that someone was indeed expelled from the University of Leipzig, although it was not Dr. von Kroninschildt but his father, (Johann) Caspar Richter. The doctor added "von Kroninschildt" to his surname probably because his family had a coat of arms with a crown on the shield. Richter was a common name in Germany, and it is likely that the doctor took the additional name to distinguish his family from so many other families.[10]

The other tradition with a "modicum of fact" involves a line in my wife's ancestry. Her family is descended from a Welshman named Henry Parry, of Pittsburgh, by his wife Sarah, traditionally said to have been a daughter of General John Cadwalader, of Philadelphia and Kent County, Maryland—a Revolutionary War hero. When I searched the Cadwalader family genealogies, I found that the general was twice married, first to Elizabeth Lloyd, a Maryland heiress, and second to Williamina Bond, of a prominent family of Maryland and Philadelphia. By Elizabeth he had three daughters, Anne, Elizabeth, and Maria, and by Williamina a daughter Frances. No Sarah. I immediately discarded the claim. Some years later I found a clue in an Allegheny County, Pennsylvania, deed book. By a preponderance of the evidence (a statement by one of Sarah's sons; the aforementioned deed book; Christ Church registers in Philadelphia; five wills made by General Cadwalader; his estate papers in Philadelphia and Kent County; and a letter from Cadwalader's son-in-law, Samuel Ringgold, to another son-in-law, Archibald McCall) I was able to show that General Cadwalader did indeed have a daughter Sarah by Anne Dingwell, his daughter Maria's nurse.[11] It is interesting that the "modicum of fact" in both the Crowninshield and Cadwalader families revolved around an illegitimate child.

As we began this chapter with a quotation from Jacobus, let us conclude it with another from the same article: "Although few traditions prove to be true in every particular, the genealogist should not, with a superior air, dismiss a tradition as unworthy of consideration. Occasionally a traditional statement is found to be very close to the truth, however misapplied or encircled with errors. Therefore, tradition should be sifted and tested, and utilized as clues, but not accepted as true until verified from contemporary documentary evidence."

Notes

1. Donald Lines Jacobus, "Tradition and Family History," *The American Genealogist*, 9:1 (July 1932; hereinafter referred to as *TAG*). This article was reprinted by Noel C. Stevenson in *The Genealogical Reader* (1958), and by the American Society of Genealogists in *Genealogical Research: Methods and Sources*, vol. 1, (Milton Rubincam, ed.), in both the 1960 and revised 1980 editions.

2. The claims were propagated as fact by Thomas Bentley Wikoff in *Anneke Jans Bogardus and Her Amsterdam Estate. Past and Present. Romance of a Dutch Maiden and its present New World Sequel. Historical, Legal, Genealogical* (Indianapolis, 1924). In *Anneke Jans Bogardus, Her Farm and How it became the Property of Trinity Church* (1896), Thomas P. Nash entitles the first chapter "The Anneke Jans Delusion for Lucre." John Reynolds Totten, in his article "Anneke Jans (1607-08?-1663), and Her Two Husbands, Roelof Jans (or Jansen) and Rev. (Domine) Everardus Bogardus and Their Descendants to the Third Generation Inclusive" (*The New York Genealogical and Biographical Record*, 56:202-03, July 1925), recites Anneke's traditional descent from William the Silent, and concludes that the story is a "mere tradition." George Olin Zabriskie, FASG, contributed to the *Record* for April and July 1973 an article, "Anneke Jans in Fact and Fiction," in which he demolishes the royal claim, and proves that the father assigned to her was the wrong man.

3. Milton Rubincam, "The German Background of the Rubincam-Revercomb Family of Pennsylvania and Virginia," *TAG*, 15:172-78 (January 1939).

4. Curiously, the Bucks County branch of the family (Rubinkam) claimed a Welsh origin, while the Virginia branch (Revercomb) was credited with a Scottish origin!

5. That is, the Protestant cantons of Switzerland.

6. This story was originally told in my article "American Families of Hessian Descent," *National Genealogical Society Quarterly* 48:78 (June 1960; hereinafter referred to as *NGSQ*).

7. Dr. Adams sent me a translation of Oswald Schott's baptismal record along with a photostat of Oswald Gutberlet's pedigree in all traceable lines to the seventeenth century. The Hessian soldier settled in New Jersey, married Agnes Mungal, and the family name was converted to "Good Bartlett" (or "Goodbartket"). For generations these Bartletts used "Good" as a middle name.

8. Netti Schreiner-Yantis, *Genealogical and Local History Books in Print* (1985), 2:1616, no. 3874. The compiler lists the genealogies of the Hessian soldiers that have been published so far.

9. Milton Rubincam, "Shakespeare's 'American Descendants,'" *NGSQ*, 47:134-35 (September 1959).

10. G. Andrews Moriarty, "The Origin of the Crowninshields," *TAG*, 25:220-23 (October 1949).

11. Milton Rubincam, "The Identity and Ancestry of Sarah, Wife of Henry Parry, of Pittsburgh, Pennsylvania," *NGSQ*, 53:181-86. See also a correction to the pedigree in "William Wood of Burlington County, New Jersey," *NGSQ*, 59:8-11 (March 1971).

CHAPTER 4

THE PROBLEM OF DATES

Dates are extremely important in genealogical research, especially in the early generations of a family when precise dates of birth, marriage, and death are not available. From various circumstances it is often possible to calculate dates. For example, if a burial record or tombstone inscription states that a certain person was so many years, months, and days old at time of death, simple arithmetic can establish the approximate date of birth. We say "approximate," for the record used as a basis may not necessarily be accurate and sometimes the records are contradictory.

We have an example of this in my maternal grandmother's family. Her uncle, Donald Sutherland, died at Bradford, Simcoe County, Ontario, Canada, on 22 November 1885 at age ninety-two years, eleven months, twelve days, according to his tombstone inscription in the Scotch Settlement graveyard at Bradford. This would place his date of birth as 1 December 1793. The local newspaper, *The South Simcoe News*, in its issue of 26 November 1885, reported that his age was ninety-one years, nine months, fifteen days, thus establishing his birth date as 10 February 1794. In his case, we are fortunate enough to have his actual birth date from the parochial register of births of Kildonan, Sutherlandshire, Scotland: 15 February 1796 (Microfilm Reel No. 101980, The Genealogical Society, Salt Lake City). He was thus eighty-nine years, nine months, twelve days old at his death.

Donald's younger brother, Alexander Sutherland (my great-grandfather), of Holland Landing, York County, Ontario, had the distinction of dying on two separate dates: 23 March 1882, according to Death Certificate No. 02079, on file in the Office of the Registrar General,

Toronto; and 25 March 1882, according to the family Bible (detached family record pages in my collections). His grandson-in-law, Duncan Bell, who provided the information to the Registrar General, gave Alexander's year of birth as 1800. This is an error; he was born at Kildonan, Sutherlandshire, 28 February 1802, as shown by both the family Bible and the above-mentioned Kildonan register of births. In a situation such as this, one cannot accept either date but must give both dates with the authority for each.

In connection with the family Bible, Alexander Sutherland's wife, Ann[3] Johnson, was daughter of Joseph Johnson, the first settler at Holland Landing. A native Philadelphian who accompanied his Loyalist family first to Nova Scotia and later to Upper Canada (now Ontario) in 1783/84, he was born on 1 October 1766 (Bible). Can we accept this date as accurate? The answer is *possibly*, perhaps *probably*, but not *certainly* without further corroboration. The Bible was printed by Robert Sears, 181 Williams Street, New York, in 1856, ninety years after Joseph Johnson's alleged date of birth. It was thus not a contemporary record of his birth. It may have been copied from an earlier record. Although many of the dates in this Bible have been confirmed from other sources, still, those before 1856 are hearsay. The point of this story is: whenever a family Bible is found containing records of birth, marriage, and death, one should confirm the records from other evidence, if possible. Note that Alexander Sutherland's birth date (28 February 1802), written over half a century later in the Bible, is corroborated by the record in the Kildonan birth register. One thing the researcher should always remember is to check the title page of the Bible to see when, by whom, and in what place it was published. If the vital records are after the date of publication, the chances are good that the entries were made contemporaneously.

The Johnson family provides us with other problems of dates. Joseph's brother, Abraham, died 28 May 1840, aged seventy-three years (no months or days stated), according to his tombstone inscription in the Cummer Burial Ground, Willowdale (now part of the city of Toronto).[1] This would make his year of birth 1767, a date accepted by his descendant.[2] m two petitions for land in Upper Canada he stated that he was the eldest son of Lawrence Johnson, the Loyalist. But if he were the older brother of Joseph Johnson, who was born in 1766 as stated in the Bible, he could not have been born in 1767. In the absence of church registers giving dates of birth or baptism for the five Johnson brothers, I have estimated that Abraham was born about 1764, and that his parents, Lawrence and Mary, were perhaps married in 1762 or 1763. In colonial times the average age of boys at marriage was 21 to 26, and of girls from 18 to 24.[3] The ages at death as given in the Bible for the parents make Lawrence born in about 1741, and his wife, a little older, in 1739.

Sometimes inexperienced genealogists, in their eagerness to latch onto notable families, completely disregard dates, with ludicrous results. Well over sixty years ago a lady published her descent from the Haines and related families of Burlington County, New Jersey.[4] Her ancestor, Richard Haines, a Quaker from Aynho, Northamptonshire, England, died at sea in 1682 aboard the ship *Amith*.[5] The author implied that he was a son of the Reverend John Haynes, an Anglican clergyman in Essex County, England, who was the son of John Haynes, colonial governor of Connecticut, by his wife, Mabel Harlakenden, a descendant of King Edward III. This would have given Richard's descendants a glorious royal ancestry. But alas! There is a chronological flaw in the claim. Mabel Harlakenden was born in 1614, and if Richard were her grandson, she would have been about 21 or 22 years old at his birth (estimated as 1636) and he would have been born at about the same time as his father!

In 1937 a book was published purporting to show the royal ancestry of George Gardiner, an early New England settler. The next year Meredith Colket virtually took this pedigree apart by demonstrating that no proof was offered for Gardiner's parentage. In fact, in the medieval portion of the volume the authors had crowded six generations into about thirty years and had indicated that a woman was married before her great-grandmother was born![6]

Even experienced genealogists have fallen into this chronological trap. Two well-known scholars published a work in 1955 that crowded seven generations into twenty-four years and showed the Right Reverend Edwin Sandys, D.D. (1516-1588), Archbishop of York, as being born thirty years before his great-great-great-great-grandmother.[7] In a work on the Carters of England and Virginia, a distinguished British genealogist, whose other books have made important contributions to Anglo-American genealogy, covered six generations in thirty-five years and made a girl born a year after her mother's death.[8]

An amusing instance of a disregard of dates is the fabricated pedigree of the House of Russell, Earls and Dukes of Bedford. Their ancestor, John Russell, who died in 1505, was declared to be Speaker of the House of Commons eighty-two years earlier! The late great English genealogist, J. Horace Round, in his expose of the pedigree, wittily remarked: "The difficulty of identifying this John, who died in 1505, with a Speaker of the House of Commons in 1423, has been always felt to be serious."[9]

A really idiotic disregard of dates appeared in 1946 in that highly useful question-and-answer paper, *Genealogy & History*. A query stated that in 1310 Hugh Sawyer was knighted for bravery by Richard Coeur-de-Lion, and that his son, Sir Robert Sawyer, was attorney to King Charles II.[10] This claim was made in all seriousness. The absurdity of the statement is realized when one remembers that over 350 years separated the "father" in 1310 and his "son" in the reign of Charles II (1660-1685). Moreover, King Richard could not have knighted anyone in 1310 because he had been killed in action in 1199. The Sawyer family must have been in a state of suspended animation!

There are many other stories that could be told of the careless handling of dates. Records of birth, marriage, and death in vital statistics offices are often in error because of lack of knowledge on the informants' part. I was helping a friend named Evelyn on her genealogy, and since one always works back from the present, I sent to the Office of Vital Statistics, State Department of Health, Frankfort, Kentucky, for a copy of her birth certificate. When it arrived we had a surprise. The date of birth was correct, the names of both parents were correct, the place of birth (Harlan County) was correct, but her name wasn't. It was recorded as Elizabeth. I've forgotten the reason for this fluke but by getting her father to sign an affidavit we submitted a delayed registration and had her name corrected to Evelyn Gertrude. When I was in Pittsburgh many years ago I obtained a copy of the death certificate of my aunt who died there in 1928. My mother, the informant, made her sister younger than she was and born in the wrong place—Toronto, instead of Holland Landing, Ontario.

Dates on tombstones have to be checked carefully with other evidence, as previously stated. But it is left to a tombstone in the Upper Burial Ground, Germantown, Philadelphia, to provide evidence that one Pennsylvania colonist attained a very advanced age: Adam Schisler died 22 December 1777, aged 969 years.[11] Actually, he was 69, but the stonecutter thought he was 96 and so inscribed it on the monument. When he discovered his mistake, he added a "9" to the "96" and filled in the first "9" so that the deceased's true age would be shown. But time has removed the filling so that according to the tombstone he had reached the age of the biblical Methuselah (969 years) at the time of his death.

Notes

1. "The Cummer Burial Ground," *The York Pioneer* (Toronto: York Pioneer and Historical Society, 1966), p. 10.

2. *The Canada Settlement, Ogle County, Illinois* (Polo, Illinois, 1939), p. 7 (article, "Our Ancestors," written by John Poole in 1912); Harriet M. Purdy, "The Lawrence Johnson Family," *Families* (organ of the Ontario Genealogical Society), 13:47 (Spring 1974).

3. Jacobus, "Dates and the Calendar," *TAG*, 9:130 (January 1933); also reprinted by Stevenson, *Genealogical Reader*, p. 13.

4. Mrs. Robert E. Baldry, *Genealogy of the Haines, Rogers, Austin, Taylor, Garwood, Reich and Hunt Families* (1922), no pagination.

5. Capt. John W. Haines, USN (Ret.), *Richard Haines and His Descendants. A Quaker Family of Burlington County, New Jersey since 1682*, 1 (1961): 37–38.

6. Meredith B. Colket, Jr., "The 'Royal Ancestry' of George Gardiner," *TAG*.

7. Arthur Adams and Frederick Lewis Weis, *The Magna Charta Sureties, 1215. The Barons Named in the Magna Charta, 1215 and Some of Their Descendants Who Settled in America, 1607-1650* (Boston, 1955), p. 95. The two later editions (1964 and 1979), edited by Walter Lee Sheppard, Jr., point out the impossibility of this pedigree, with the notation, "This line is NOT an acceptable one." Although Dr. Adams's name is on the title page, Dr. Weis was the preparer of the pedigrees.

8. Noel Currer-Briggs, *The Carters of Virginia: Their English Ancestry* (Chicester, Sussex, England, 1979), pp. 93 (Table 1), and 100 (unnumbered table).

9. J. Horace Round, *Studies in Peerage and Family History* (New York: Longmans, Green & Company, and Westminster: Archibald Constable & Company, Ltd., 1901), p. 263.

10. *Genealogy & History*, 6:item no. 10928 (15 January 1946), and 7:item no. 11130 (15 March 1946, my reply).

11. Transcript of Upper Burial Ground inscriptions, Genealogical Society of Pennsylvania, Philadelphia. Adam Schisler (Schussler) was probably the man of that name who landed in Philadelphia on 16 September 1738, from the ship *Queen Elizabeth*. On one of the passenger lists of that vessel his age is given as thirty, thus making him born in 1708. This would be the right year of birth for Adam Schisler who died in 1777, at age sixty-nine. (See Strassburger and Hinke, *Pennsylvania German Pioneers*, 1966 reprint, 1:217, 218, 220.)

CHAPTER 5

THE 1752 CALENDAR CHANGE

O ne of the most important problems facing the beginner in genealogical research relates to the calendars in use during the colonial period of our history, at least prior to 1752. One must understand the difference between the Julian and the Gregorian calendars, the reason for the switch from one to the other, the double-dating system, and so on.

In 46-45 B.C. Gaius Julius Caesar, *Pontifex Maximus* and Dictator, with the assistance of Sosiegenes, astronomer and mathematician from Alexandria, Egypt, reformed the Roman republican calendar. It was computed that the solar year—the time it takes for the Earth to revolve around the sun—was 365 days, six hours. Three years, each consisting of 365 days, were to be followed by a fourth (or leap) year of 366 days. But this was slightly over eleven minutes too much, or about one day in 128 years.

In the year 325 Emperor Constantine I (The Great) presided over an ecumenical council at Nicaea, in Bithynia, an ancient region in northwestern Asia Minor. (Nicaea is now named Iznik, in Turkey.) Among the problems considered by the 220 bishops in attendance was the date of Easter, which had been in controversy for many years. They established the vernal equinox, then falling on 21 March, as the basis for determining the date of the most sacred festival in the Christian Church. The dates of many religious holidays are based on Easter. The Julian calendar was adopted by the Council of Nicaea.

During the Middle Ages astronomers and mathematicians were aware of the discrepancies in the Julian calendar. Several efforts were made to reform it but nothing came of them. By the sixteenth century, calendar dates were ahead of actual time by ten days, and the vernal equinox had shifted to 11 March.

When Ugo Buoncompagni ascended the papal throne on 13 May 1572 as Gregory XIII, he took up the question of reforming the calendar, and succeeded where his predecessors had failed. Acting on the advice of Aloysius Lilius (Luigi Lilio Ghiraldi), Neapolitan physician and mathematician, and Bavarian Jesuit and mathematician Christopher Clavius, he issued a decree in March 1582, promulgating the new calendar called in his honor Gregorian (also known as New Style, or N.S., just as the Julian calendar is called Old Style, or O.S.). He directed that the day after the Feast of St. Francis (of Assisi), 4 October, should be reckoned as 15 October 1582. Consequently, the next vernal equinox fell properly on 21 March instead of on the eleventh of the month. Pope Gregory ordered that no century year should be considered a leap year unless it was exactly divisible by 400. Thus 1700, 1800, and 1900 would be common years but 1600 and 2000 would be leap years.

The Catholic counties of Europe adopted the Gregorian calendar as soon as possible after copies of the decree had reached them. The Protestant countries were slow to follow suit, not being willing to obey a Pope's orders. The Protestant states of the Holy Roman Empire, by order of the Diet (Parliament) at Regensburg, dropped eleven days from the 19th to the 29th of February 1700, so that 18 February immediately became 1 March. Lists of the countries and the dates when they converted to the new calendar are contained in Archibald F. Bennett, *A Guide for Genealogical Research* (1951), p. 323, and Ethel W. Williams, *Know Your Ancestors* (1972), pp. 35-36. A much more comprehensive list is published by Kenneth L. Smith in *A Practical Guide to Dating Systems for Genealogists* (1983), pp. 7-9. The latter not only gives the major countries but breaks the list down into fine segments. For instance, we learn that the bishopric of Basel, in Switzerland, converted on 31 October 1583, but the city of Basel did not do so until 12 January 1701. The Orthodox countries of Russia and Greece converted as late as 1918 and 1923, respectively.

Scotland, while still a separate kingdom before its union with England under James VI and I, converted in 1600 by order of the Privy Council. England and her colonies finally fell in line when Parliament passed an act in 1751 ordering that the Gregorian calendar be adopted for all legal and public business. By that time the difference between the Julian and Gregorian calendars amounted to eleven days, and it was therefore further enacted that the day following 2 September 1752 should be called 14 September. The people did not understand the reason for this; they thought they were being deprived of eleven days of their lives and rioted, screaming, "Give us back our eleven days!"

Many persons living in England and the colonies at the time the calendar was changed in 1752 rectified their birth dates. A case often cited in genealogical manuals and handbooks is that of George Washington, who was born on 11 February 1731 according to the Julian or Old Style Calendar, but when the change occurred he celebrated his birthday thereafter on 22 February.

New Year's Day has been observed on different dates throughout history. The ancient Roman republican calendar began the year on 1 March, but after 153 B.C., New Year's Day was changed to 1 January and this was confirmed by Julius Caesar's calendar. In England our Anglo-Saxon ancestors celebrated 25 December as New Year's Day, and William the Conqueror (1066-1087) decreed 1 January as the first day of the year. But most Christian countries from early medieval times had recognized 25 March (Lady Day or Annunciation Day) as New Year's, and in time England fell into step and observed the same day, down to 1752. Although the year began on the twenty-fifth day of the month, all of March was considered the first month, April the second month, May the third month, June the fourth month, and so on to the twelfth month, February. The names of certain months are reminiscent of Roman history. September, now our ninth month, was so called because it was the seventh (from Latin *septem*, seven). October, the tenth month, was the eighth (Latin *octo*), and December, the twelfth month, was the tenth (Latin *decem*). The Roman month Quintilis was renamed July in honor of Caesar, and Sextilis was changed to August to satisfy the vanity of Caesar's great-nephew Augustus, the first Roman emperor.

The year beginning on 25 March was known as ecclesiastical, legal, or civil year. Even so, the first of January had been considered (since Norman times) as the beginning of the historical year. As a result, it was customary to use a double-dating system between 1 January and 25 March: thus, George Washington was born on 11 February 1731/32, to show that he was born on the 11th of the month in 1731 but in 1732 under the Gregorian calendar. This was not always done in the records and one may find records that give only the number of the old year up through the 24th of March, and the next day adding one to the number of the year.

This can cause complications. Jacobus cites the case of Ephraim Burr who, according to his tombstone inscription, died 29 April 1776, aged seventy-six years and thirteen days. When one subtracts his age from his death date one gets 16 April 1700 as his date of birth. His baptismal record is 14 April 1700, before his supposed birth date! But one now must subtract eleven days to get his birth date by the Julian calendar: 5 April 1700, nine days prior to his baptism.

Walter Goodwin Davis, in *The Ancestry of Joseph Waterhouse, 1754-1837, of Standish, Maine* (Portland, 1949), p. 67, tells the story of Dr. George Gains Brewster. Mr. Davis discusses three printed versions of a family record made by a seventeenth century woman of Portsmouth, New Hampshire, Mary (Sherburne) Sloper (an ancestress of Dr. Brewster). "Two entries in version II brought a blush to Dr. Brewster's cheek," Mr. Davis writes. "'Bridget Sloper was married unto John Knight 29th March 1684' and 'John Knight was borne 29th January 1684.' Totally unaware that the year began on March 25, it seemed to him shameful but undeniable that small John entered the world two months before his parents' marriage (instead of ten months thereafter), so the shocking fact of John's existence was omitted altogether in versions III and I." We will meet again with Dr. Brewster in our account of fraudulent pedigrees.

Another example: Samuel Haines, of Northampton Township, Burlington County, New Jersey, made his will on "2.11 mo." (January) 1748/49. It was probated 26 January 1748. As the family genealogist comments: "This is one instance where the date of probate appears to be earlier than the date of the will, due to the fact that legally the year remained 1748 until March 24, while historically the year was 1749 after January 1." (Capt. John W. Haines, USN, Ret., *Richard Haines and His Descendants, A Quaker Family of Burlington County, New Jersey, since 1682*, 1:130.)

The aforementioned will brings us to the system of Quaker dating. From the beginning of the history of the Society of Friends in the middle of the seventeenth century, the Quakers abhorred the names of the months and of the days, because of their pagan origin. Instead of naming the months and days, the Friends numbered them. Before 1752 they called March the first month, April the second, and so on. Sunday was the first day, Monday the second day, Tuesday the third day, etc. One Chester County, Pennsylvania, court record begins quaintly: "Att a Court held att Chester for ye County of Chester ye 3rd day of ye 1st week of ye 8th moneth 1688."

We have been considering the calendar only as it was used in the English colonies. Holland adopted the Gregorian calendar on 1 January 1583; it was in use in New Netherland for some forty years. After the English conquest in 1664, when the province became New York, the Julian calendar was instituted. Those whose ancestors lived in the French and Spanish colonies must remember that the Gregorian calendar was in force in those territories.

The history of our calendar is a fascinating one, and the shift from the Julian to the Gregorian calendar involves complications that the genealogist must learn to handle. We have touched on the subject only briefly; the reader would be well advised to study two articles that go into considerable detail: "The 1752 Calendar Change," by Paul W. Prindle, in *TAG*, 40:246-48 (October 1964); and "Genealogy and the Calendar," by George B. Wilson, in the *Maryland Magazine of Genealogy* (Baltimore: Maryland Historical Society), 1:13-20 (Fall 1978). Mention has already been made of Kenneth L. Smith's *A Practical Guide to Dating Systems for Genealogists* (Columbus, Ohio, 1983). He discusses not only the Julian and Gregorian calendars but also the French republican calendar, in force from 1792 to 1805 in France and territories under French dominion during those years. As a great many European dates are based on certain feast days, his list of such days on pp. 29-115 is invaluable. For those who wish to pursue the history of the calendar in depth, I recommend P. W. Wilson's *The Romance of the Calendar* (1937); a valuable chronology from *ca.* 1800 B.C. to 1936 concludes the work.

CHAPTER 6

MORE CONFUSION: SAME NAME, SAME PLACE, SAME TIME

A nother problem that frequently confronts the genealogist involves people of the same name and approximately the same age residing in close proximity. It is bad enough when there are only two people of the same name, as in the case of Samuel Tuttle and Samuel Tuthill, cited earlier in connection with another pitfall. But if there is a multiplicity of persons bearing the same name, one has to exert all of his genealogical skill to separate them and put each in his or her proper setting.

One of the neatest pieces of genealogical detective work that I have seen is contained in Mrs. John E. Barclay's article "Five Jonathan Dunhams Untangled," in *TAG*, 44:218-23 (October 1968). The story begins with the Reverend Jonathan Dunham, of Dukes County, Massachusetts, who made his will on 28 June 1717. He named his sons Jonathan, Eleazer, Gershom, and Samuel, daughter Parker, widow, and son Daniel and wife. "As we read this will," Mrs. Barclay writes, "we get the impression all are living since none are called deceased, but such was not the case. Gershom, Daniel and Hannah, were living and left estates (Dukes County probate records) but Jonathan, Jr., Eleazer and Samuel all died several years before date of the will, proof of which will be found as follows:

"Samuel[3] died unmarried the latter part of 1701. He was living 15 June 1698, date of Dukes County Deeds 1:136, but is called deceased in Deeds 1:403 dated 30 December 1701. The Rev. Isaac Dunham in his genealogy gives a specific date of death: 15 June 1689—definitely an error.

"Eleazer[3] died unmarried near 10 October 1710, the date Plymouth County Deeds 8:175 and 8:144 were recorded. He was not the father of Ebenezer, Ephraim, Samuel, Stephen, and Manassah, as given by the genealogy (p. 143). Their parentage can be proven otherwise."

The genealogy of the five Jonathan Dunhams descending from the Reverend Jonathan can best be shown in chart form:

Jonathan Dunham, Jr. (son of the Reverend Jonathan); married

(1)	(2) Hester (Norton) Huxford, widow
Jonathan, Jr.; died at Sharon, Connecticut, 22 February 1744/5; married Mary Spencer	Jonathan; died near 13 February 1745/6, at Edgartown, Massachusetts (a year after his half-brother of the same name); married Judith Luce (who did not marry his half-brother Jonathan, as stated by earlier genealogists)
Jonathan, Jr.; died at Sharon, 29 October 1740; married Elizabeth _____	Jonathan, Jr.; living on 27 November 1747

Mrs. Barclay worked out this difficult problem by a thorough study and analysis of probate and land records of Massachusetts and Connecticut. She corrected serious errors that had occurred in the Rev. Isaac Dunham's *The Dunham Genealogy* and in Col. Charles E. Banks's version in *Families of Martha's Vineyard*. The student of genealogy would be well advised to read Mrs. Barclay's article as an example of excellent genealogical research and writing.

Dr. George E. McCracken worked on an interesting problem involving the Gillett family of Windsor, Connecticut. In his article "Too Many Jonathan Gilletts in Windsor, Connecticut," *TAG*, 56:72-79 (April 1980), he listed seventeen men by the name of Jonathan Gillett who lived in Windsor from before 1677 to 1777. These included "four pairs of brothers who never met each other, the elder of each pair having died before the birth of the younger." The Gilletts were confused in Dr. Henry R. Stiles's well-known *History of Ancient Windsor* (2nd ed., 1892, reprinted 1976). In one case Dr. Stiles received a shock when he thought that Jonathan Gillett, born 5 July 1716, had married on 28 April 1759 his own daughter Rachel (widow of Stephen Goodrich). Dr. McCracken shows that Rachel was not the daughter of her husband, but of another

Jonathan Gillett. Rachel was thus the second cousin once removed, not the daughter, of her husband. The main purpose of the article is to distinguish the families of Capt. Jonathan Gillett (1716—after 1785) and Jonathan Gillett (1738-79) who had two sons named Jonathan.

A statement in *The Old United Empire Loyalists' List* (originally published in 1885 at Toronto, reprinted by the Genealogical Publishing Company, Inc., Baltimore, Md., 1969 and 1976) caused me to run after the wrong Lawrence Johnson. It reads: "Johnson, Laurence. H. District. Served in Col. Robinson's Regiment." I knew that my great-great-great-grandfather, Lawrence Johnson, a Philadelphia Loyalist (whose family was mentioned in an earlier chapter) resided in the Home District, which later consisted of the counties of York and Simcoe in Upper Canada (now Ontario).

I was delighted to learn about which regiment my ancestor served in. I knew that Col. Beverley Robinson, a Virginian long settled in New York State, commanded the Loyal American Regiment. The muster rolls of that unit are among the photostats of the Loyalist Corps in the Manuscripts Division of the Library of Congress. I searched them eagerly, and found Lawrence's complete record: when and where he enlisted, where he served, when he was sick, when he was captured by "the rebels," and approximately when he was released and returned to his regiment.

I pursued further research in the Archives of Ontario at Toronto. And then came disillusionment. I had violated my own dictum: "Don't believe what you see in print!" There were two Loyalist Lawrence Johnsons. From the Upper Canada Land Petitions (photocopies of which I received from the Dominion Archives, Ottawa, at a later date), I learned that my Lawrence indeed did serve with the king's forces in America but as a wagoner; the regiment in which he served was not named. It was necessary to work on both Lawrences in order to distinguish one from the other. I found by research at Toronto and later by correspondence with the Norfolk Historical Society at Simcoe, Norfolk County, Ontario, that the other Lawrence lived in the area called the London District (*not* the Home District, where my forebear resided). I have a photocopy of the draft of a petition he wrote in which he described his service in Colonel Robinson's regiment.

How did it happen that my ancestor was credited with the military service of his namesake, who, incidentally, was from New York State? The misnamed "Old U.E.L. List" is not the official list of Loyalists; it was a list compiled for the Crown Lands Department and included many Loyalists but also many settlers and discharged German mercenary soldiers. Whoever compiled the list was also scanning muster rolls, noted a Lawrence Johnson in Robinson's regiment, and assumed he was the man

of that name who lived in the Home District. The official list of
Loyalists is known as the Executive Council List.

In his article "Interpreting Genealogical Records," *TAG*, 10:2 et seq.
(July 1933), reprinted in Stevenson's *The Genealogical Reader*, Jacobus
tells us about five men named John Hall who lived in the same town
contemporaneously; they were known as John Hall, Sr., Jr., 3rd, 4th, and
5th. When Sr. went to his reward, Jr. was promoted to Sr. and each of
the others went up a step. They obtained their labels strictly according to
age.

When I had an assignment with the Valley Forge Park Commission
to compile records of men who served at Valley Forge during the ter-
rible winter of 1777-78, I found three men named John Rawlings serving
simultaneously in Capt. Richard Weare's Company, 3rd New Hampshire
Regiment. They were designated in the company muster rolls as John
Rawlings; John Rawlings, 2nd; and John Rawlings, 3rd. These were ar-
bitrary designations and were not given to them because of their respec-
tive ages. (For details, see my article "Three John Rawlings in the
Revolutionary War," *NGSQ*, 32:113, December 1948).

Many more cases could be cited, including instances where men of
the same name living in the same community at the same time married
women bearing the same name, thus causing their descendants infinite
problems trying to sort them out and make a correct identification. The
reader is referred to Noel C. Stevenson's work, *Genealogical Evidence:
A Guide to the Standard of Proof Relating to Pedigrees, Ancestry, Heir-
ship, and Family History* (Laguna Hills, Calif., Aegean Park Press, 1979)
pp. 11-28, for a detailed discussion of the many problems of identification.

CHAPTER 7

INTERPRETATION OF TERMS

Some years ago a woman told me she was going to search naval records at the National Archives. She said she had found a statement that her Virginia ancestor was a yeoman, which, she explained, meant he was a petty officer in the Navy. I agreed that yeoman is a naval rating, but suggested she would do well to go to the State Library of Virginia at Richmond to search microfilms of the records of her ancestor's county, for in his case I was confident he was a farmer.

In the seventeenth and eighteenth centuries our ancestors' wills, deeds, and other records contained many words that had different shades of meaning from the same words used today. In England and colonial America, a yeoman was a man owning or cultivating a small estate—in other words, a freeholder under the rank of gentleman.[1] Sometimes we find an ancestor who is called a "husbandman." This is an archaic term for a man who tills and cultivates the soil, in other words, a farmer.[2]

We mentioned "gentleman" above. Our modern dictionaries tell us that a gentleman is "a man who is honorable, courteous, and considerate."[3] But in English and early American history a gentleman was a man entitled to bear a coat of arms; he ranked below the nobleman. He did not perform manual labor or engage in trade. He owned an estate from which he derived his income.[4] George Washington and Robert E. Lee, belonging to large landowning families and bearing coats of arms, were described as "gentlemen." The usual abbreviation in records was Gent. The wife of a gentleman was a gentlewoman.

In the nineteenth century the word gentleman was often used in another context—to denote a man who had retired from business. In 1842 the city directory of Philadelphia listed my great-great-uncle, Joseph Rubincam, recently retired as head of a firm of manufacturing confectioners, as "gent." I have seen it used in other city directories to designate a retired businessman.

In the seventeenth and eighteenth centuries some of our ancestors were called "Mr." and "Mrs." These titles were reserved for persons of social position. Mr. (Mister) was originally Master. In colonial times it was applied strictly to those whose families belonged to the landed gentry, to clergymen, and to public officials who were entitled to it.[5] One of the earliest settlers of Watertown, Massachusetts (who arrived in 1635), was a man who was called in the records variously as William Swayne, Gentleman, and Mr. William Swayne, thus denoting his high position. Persons so designated were accorded pews nearest the pulpit in the churches and meeting houses. They were treated with great respect.

The term Mrs. (originally Mistress) is a pitfall in itself. It was applied to both married and unmarried women and girls of a social position.[6] So, if one finds an ancestress or other female relative called "Mrs." So-and-So one must not jump to the conclusion that she was a married woman.

In New England we come across the terms Goodman and Goodwife (shortened to Goody). They were people of substance who ranked below the gentry. Jacobus tells about a silly error made by the genealogist of a Dunham family. He found his ancestor called Goodman Dunham, and jumped to the conclusion that he was John Goodman of the *Mayflower*. The compiler of the book did not understand that "Goodman" designated the position his forebear held in the community. There was no connection with the Goodman family.

Terms of relationship as found in the records can also be vexing. The words "brother," "cousin," "uncle," "nephew," and "son," may not have had the same meaning in colonial times that they have today. A brother may indeed have been a full brother, but he may also have been a half-brother, a stepbrother, a brother by adoption, a brother-in-law, or a brother in the church. On 15 March 1760 Thomas Pyatt, of Piscataway, Middlesex County, New Jersey, made his will. He left a large number of bequests to relatives, including one hundred pounds to "my brother-in-law, Joseph Drake." How was Drake his brother-in-law? He wasn't, according to the way we use the term today. His mother, Ruth, *nee* Fitz-Randolph, was married first to Joseph Drake, Sr., by whom she had a son, Joseph Drake, and second to James Pyatt, by whom she had a flock of children, including the testator, Thomas Pyatt. Thus, Joseph Drake, the inheritor of one hundred pounds, and Thomas Pyatt, the testator, were half-brothers.

If a man referred to his "cousin," he may have been mentioning his uncle or nephew, for they were interchangeable terms in those days. My last German ancestor, Pastor Johann Philipp Rubenkam, in a letter to the ecclesiastical authorities of Hessen-Kassel, reported the death of his "cousin," Johann Gleim, Pastor of Wanfried—who was not his cousin but his maternal uncle. I have a copy of a document from the Hessian State Archives at Marburg in which Landgrave Wilhelm the Elder of Hessen-Rheinfels referred to his nephew and co-ruler, Wilhelm the Younger, as his "cousin." The habit of calling uncles and nephews "cousins" was as prevalent in Europe and England as in the American colonies.

The word "nephew" is a sticky one, for it does not always refer to the son of one's brother or sister. It is derived from the Latin word *nepos*, meaning grandson, and there are cases when it was used in its original sense.[7] John Frederick Dorman, in *The Farish Family of Virginia and Its Forebears* (1969), quotes on pp. 84-86 the text of the will of John Hays of Augusta (later Rockbridge) County, Virginia, dated 25 December 1750, in which, besides his children, he names "my nephew John Hays Junr.," "my nephew Rebecca Hays," "my nephew Rebecky Guines," and "my nephew Robert Lust." These were not his nephews or nieces but his grandchildren. In medieval times the word nephew was often used for the illegitimate son of a Pope or other ecclesiastic. The word niece (Latin *neptis*) originally meant granddaughter. I have not seen it so used in American documents, but in 1508 it was used to designate a female relative.[8]

We are accustomed to refer to an illegitimate son or daughter as "natural" son or daughter, but in the seventeenth and eighteenth centuries the term did not necessarily have this connotation. It usually signified a son or daughter by blood and did not imply illegitimacy.

When a man mentioned "my now wife" in his will, he was not implying that he had been married previously. He was referring to the woman who was his wife at the time he drew up the will, as opposed to someone he might marry at a later date. The purpose was often to safeguard a bequest for the issue of his present ("now") wife. If she should die during his lifetime, it might very well be that he did not want a certain bequest to go to a second wife. Of course, it is always possible that he did have an earlier wife, but the genealogist must investigate all circumstances to determine the facts.

Very often in the records a man (and sometimes a woman) was designated as "Senior" or "Junior." This did not imply a father/son relationship, as it so often does today. Two cousins bearing the same name could be called "Senior" and "Junior" because of their ages. Uncle and nephew could carry the same designation. My ancestor John Woolston, a prominent figure in the old province of West New Jersey, was accompanied to America by John Woolston, Jr. Most genealogists (myself included, early in my research career) assumed they were father and son. As John, Sr., married Hannah Cooper in New Jersey, the assumption was made that John, Jr, was the senior John's son by an unknown English wife. Nothing could be further from the truth. The researches of a descendant proved conclusively that they were uncle and nephew—John, Jr., being son of his uncle John's brother, William Woolston, who died in England.[9]

Occupations mentioned in the old records can be baffling. In *The Source: A Guidebook of American Genealogy*, edited by Arlene Eakle and Johni Cerny (Salt Lake City: Ancestry Publishing, 1984), p. 342, we find a list of sixty-seven "Old Trades and Occupations." Among them are "Ale-draper" (innkeeper), "Backster/baxter" (originally a female baker, later used for either sex), "Barker" (tanner of leather), "Brewster" (a female brewer), "Cobbler" (a repairer of shoes), "Cordwainer" (a maker of good quality shoes), "Dexter" (a dyer), "Flesher" (a butcher), "Fletcher" (a maker of and dealer in arrows, and occasionally in bows and arrows), "Hind" (farm laborer; household or domestic servant), "Roper" (a rope and net maker), "Salter" (a maker and dealer in salt, a drysalter), "Scrivener" (a clerk specializing in drawing up bonds), "Smith" (a metal worker; the blacksmith worked in iron, the tinsmith in tin, also goldsmith, silversmith, etc.), "Webster" (a weaver), "Wright" (constructor, e.g. wheelwright, shipwright). Many of these occupations were later adopted as surnames.

We all know that the word "spinster" has two meanings: a woman who spins fibers into thread, and an unmarried woman, especially one who remains single beyond the ordinary marrying age, what the Germans call *eine Alte Jungfrau*, an old maid. But a recent study by Eugene A. Stratton, FASG ("A Note on Terminology: Spinster, An Indicator of Legal Status," *TAG*, 61:167-70, January/April 1986), demonstrates that in the eighteenth and early nineteenth century, spinster was also used to designate wives and widows. Moreover, in the examples cited many of the "spinsters" were engaged in transactions on their own behalf, such as selling or giving land they had received in their own right, or acquiring land in their own right. He finds a new definition of spinster, namely, "a woman legally capable of transacting business or otherwise acting in her own behalf."

Sometimes one finds an ancestor with two surnames separated by the word alias. Today we associate that word with criminals who use several "aliases" while conducting unlawful activities. However, it is common in England for an individual or family to have two surnames separated by the "alias." Parish registers often used it to indicate illegitimacy, the putative father's name and the mother's surname, with "alias" in between. Sometimes it meant an inheritance—a man marrying an heiress and adding her name to his, separated by "alias." In other cases a man whose wife or mother belonged to a distinguished family might assume the additional name, again indicated by "alias."

A good example is the history of Oliver Cromwell's family. His great-grandfather, a Welshman named Morgan Williams (formerly Morgan ap William), married the sister of Thomas Cromwell, the famous minister of Henry VIII, who, like so many of that king's supporters and foes, lost his head (1540). Their son, Richard, called himself Cromwell alias Williams, and in time the Williams was dropped and the name Cromwell retained. Richard's grandson, the Lord Protector Oliver, occasionally used "alias Williams," as in his marriage contract—but for the most part he was known as Cromwell.[10]

The well-known Custis family of Virginia may have originally been called Cliffe. John Smithier, of Arlington, Gloucester County, England, made his will on 16 February 1618; he made bequests to Henry Custis *als* Cliffe, Emond Custis *als* Cliffe, and John Custis *als* Cliffe.[11] When I was doing research on the Dutch and Belgian branches of the Custis family I was unable to determine why Edmond and John Custis *als* Cliffe, the ancestors of the Virginia line, bore this double-barrelled name.[12]

On 19 April 1750 Matthew Erwin of Augusta County, Virginia, made his will. He had no sons but he was blessed with seven daughters. He was determined that his daughters' posterity should know their identity. Two of his daughters were then unmarried, but he identified his married daughters as Gennet Erwin alias Johnson, Joan Erwin alias Jameson, Mary Erwin alias Francis, Elinor Erwin alias Patterson, and Ann Erwin alias Anderson.[13]

Gideon Jennings came to Orangeburg Township in South Carolina in 1736 with his wife and two sons. When he was buried in 1750 the clergyman who recorded the event described him as "an old Protestant Italian Liver in this Township." Six years later when his wife, Ursula, was buried, the pastor became more explicit; she was called the "widow of Gideon Zannini alias Jennings later of Orangeburgh deceased."[14] Their descendants became prominent and married members of the old South Carolina families. It isn't known if Gideon was an Englishman who went to Italy, took the name Zannini, then resumed his original name when he came to the colonies; or whether he was an Italian named Zannini who changed his name to Jennings to make it easier for the English settlers in Orangeburg to pronounce.

The use of "alias" was prevalent in Europe as well as in England and the colonies. The German word is *genannt* (called, alias) and is borne by such families as Boyneburg *genannt* Hohenstein and Schutzbar *genannt* Milchling, and many others.[15] The French word is *dit* (called, alias) and appears very frequently in France and her colonies. For instance, in

French Canada we find such names as Prejean dit Presseau and Huppe dit Lagroix.[16] In Louisiana records researchers find many names of colonists with two surnames separated by dit.

When some people find their ancestors mentioned as "servants," they feel they were socially inferior. Such was not the case. When a boy was apprenticed to learn a trade he was called a "servant" during the seven-year period of his apprenticeship. The man to whom he was apprenticed was his "master" for that period. He had to supply the lad with food and clothing, and to give him a certain amount of education. Often girls would enter the household of a neighbor to perform a variety of services. The fact that they were called "servants" did not demean their dignity or indicate a low social status.

When I was a boy, I read in the genealogy of the Potts family that my great-great-grandmother's older half-brother, Capt. Joseph Potts, a Revolutionary War veteran, became deranged in 1777. I felt so sorry for dear old Uncle Joe who had lost his reason—until I finally learned that deranged was a military term meaning that he had served his tour of duty and was no longer needed.

And what do you think of George Kirby, of the city of Herefore, England, who said in his will, dated 7 April 1609, that he was "crazy, yet of perfect memory"?[17] He was not confessing that he was insane; the word crazy in those days was used to show that he was ill, in feeble health.

Notes

1. *The Shorter Oxford English Dictionary*, prepared by William Little, H. W. Fowler, Jessie Coulson, revised and edited by C. T. Onions (3rd ed., 1973), p. 2589.

2. Ibid., p. 1000.

3. *Macmillan Contemporary Dictionary* (1979), p. 428.

4. *Shorter Oxford English Dictionary*, p. 843.

5. Ibid., p. 1337.

6. Ibid.

7. Ibid., p. 1395

8. Ibid., p. 1402.

9. Jane W. T. Brey, "The Family of Thomas Ollive of Wellingborough, Northamptonshire, and of Burlington County, West Jersey," *The Pennsylvania Genealogical Magazine*, 17 (1972):151-53. In my article "John Woolston," *Proceedings of the New Jersey Historical Society*, 59:192-97 (July 1941), I fell into the old trap of calling John Woolston, Sr. and Jr., father and son.

10. Antonia Fraser, *Cromwell: The Lord Protector* (New York, 1973), p. 8.

11. Henry F. Waters, A. M., *Genealogical Gleanings in England* (Boston, 1901), 1:700.

12. Milton Rubincam, "The Nobel Custis Family of the Netherlands and Belgium, Cadet Branch of Custis of England and Virginia," *NGSQ*, 30:75-78 (June 1942).

13. Augusta County (Virginia) Will Book 3:178-80 (Virginia State Library).

14. A. S. Sallee, Jr., *The History of Orangeburgh County, South Carolina, From the Earliest Settlement to the Close of the Revolutionary War* (Orangeburg, 1898), pp. 195 and 202.

15. Milton Rubincam, "A German Ancestor Table: Johann Philipp Rubenkam and Margaretha Catharina Sartorius," *The Genealogist*, 5:195, 197, 207, etc. (1984).

16. Thomas J. Laforest, *Our French-Canadian Ancestors* (1984), p. 223.

17. Noel Currer-Briggs, *Virginia Settlers and English Adventurers* (Baltimore, 1970), p. 139 (item no. 289).

CHAPTER 8

THE PROBLEM OF
SURNAMES

Surnames can be misleading. An American family with an English name may find that its origin is rooted in continental Europe. The Seeley family of Upstate New York was originally French Usilie. In Lancaster County, Pennsylvania, one family named Carpenter does not trace its origin to England. Edwin Sawyer Walker's *Genealogical Notes of the Carpenter Family...* (1897) shows that its pioneer ancestor was Heinrich Zimmermann (which means "carpenter") who came from Wattenwyl, district of Seftigen, canton Bern, Switzerland. Many Baker families are of German descent, the name originally being Becker or Backer (meaning "baker"). Many Smith families were formerly called Schmidt.

Rosalie Fellows Bailey's *Dutch Systems in Family Naming: New York-New Jersey* (NGS Special Publication 12, 1954, p. 9) demonstrates the origin of the Cooper family of Bergen County, New Jersey: Dutch Kuyper (meaning "cooper") descended from a certain Claes Janszen from Purmerendt in North Holland, who was in New Amsterdam by 1656. In his article "That Genealogical Quagmire: New Jersey" (*NGSQ*, 48:59-71, June 1960), Dr. Kenn Stryker-Rodda has a section entitled "Confusion of Names," in which he shows problems relating to American families of European origin. The Cole family, for instance, was once Dutch Kool (pronounced the same), and a Sharp-Sharpe family of Hunterdon County once gloried in the German Scharffenstein or Sharpenstyn.

British names also have undergone unusual transformations, such as Stephenson, occasionally reduced to Stebbings, and Phimister-Phemister, called Feamster in Virginia. Welsh names derived from patronymics include Parry (from ap Harri, son of Harry) and Bowen (ab Owen, son of Owen). Persons who trace their names to Scottish ancestors have a problem of identity, especially in the Highlands. Very often a family belonging to one clan would seek the protection of the chief of another clan and assume that chief's surname as its own. Dr. George F. Black, in *The Surnames of Scotland: Their Origin, Meaning, and History* (New York, 1948), p. xxxvii, writes: "The settlement of a powerful family within the Highland border was followed by the sudden spread of their name throughout the neighboring glens. The Gordons were hardly settled in Strathbolgy when the whole country around was full of men calling themselves Gordon."

Sounds are frequently interchangeable, such as "b" and "p," "d" and "t," and "f" and "v." This occurs especially in families of German origin: Dambach became Tambach, Voigt was changed to Focht, Brumbach became Brumbaugh and Brownback, Rubincam of Pennsylvania's branch in Virginia is Revercomb, and so on. I saw one census record where Achenbach was written Achingback!

The letters "g," "c," and "k" are also interchangeable. My kinsman the late Col. Calvin I. Kephart traced his ancestry to an immigrant named Heinrich Gebhart. A Southern family of this name uses the form Capehart.

It happens sometimes that an unusual Christian name will indicate the family to which a person belongs. An example is a family of Maxwell that settled an Albemarle and Augusta counties, Virginia, in the early eighteenth century and in the nineteenth century migrated to Jefferson County, Indiana. The name Bezaleel was prominent among its members. Thus, a Maxwell with Bezaleel in his family might reasonably be expected to descend from the Virginia Revolutionary War veteran Bezaleel Maxwell, or from his uncle Bezaleel, or from his cousin Bezaleel. But even this uncommon name is not a guarantee of kinship. An Ohio Maxwell family with some of its members named Bezaleel in the nineteenth century has been traced to a Pennsylvania Maxwell family with no known connection with the Virginia-Indiana line.

We have no easy solution to the problem of surnames. All the researcher can do is to collect every scrap of information bearing the subject, analyze it, and, based on the preponderance of the evidence, hopefully arrive at correct conclusions.

CHAPTER 9

THE YEARNING FOR ROYAL ANCESTRY

During my long career as book reviewer for the *National Genealogical Society Quarterly* (since 1942) I have seen many books claiming descent from royal and noble families. Some of the claims are valid, others are rubbish. Considering that we deposed our king in 1776, it is amazing that so many people want to claim kinship with him, even if they have to go back to the twelfth or fourteenth century to do so.

I was introduced to the subject at any early age. In 1893 Daniel Kolb Cassel published *A Genea-Biographical History of the Rittenhouse Family and all its Branches in America.* Most families are content to have just one male line origin. But Mr. Cassel endowed the Rittenhouses with two male lines of descent: one from the noble von Rittershausen family of Westphalia and the other from the splendid Imperial House of Habsburg. Thus, he gave descendants of pioneer Wilhelm Rittinghausen (Rittenhouse) (1644-1708) their choice of ancestors. I chose the royal line—it was so much more interesting! As a result, I papered the walls of my room with charts of my "descent" from Rudolf of Habsburg, Maximilian I, Charles V, Maximilian II, the Kings of France and England, and the Castilian sovereigns. Eventually, as I became proficient in research, learned to read French and German, and dug deeply into the history of the Habsburgs, I realized that this was one of the falsest claims ever perpetrated on an American family. I now refer to the above-named rulers as my "former ancestors." I certainly hated to give up Ferdinand and Isabella, though; I felt that as long as I had them in my ancestry my family had played a significant part in the discovery of America.

The Rittenhouse claim was first exposed by Mrs. Olive Barrick Rowland in 1935 in her book on the Sutton and Rittenhouse families. In his article "Rittinhouse Genealogy Debunked" (*NGSQ*, 26:105-10, December 1938), Col. Calvin I. Kephart analyzed the name and determined that the family was probably derived from a Rodinghausen or Rettinghausen family, since eighteenth-century documents in Pennsylvania gave the name as Rettinhouse, among other variations. I thoroughly exploded the royal claim in my biography of William Rittenhouse, published in 1959 by the Pennsylvania German Society, by proving genealogically the impossibility of Rittenhouse's descent from Emperor Maximilian II, who died in 1576. Even so, some descendants of the family still believe in their "royal ancestry."

Americans are not alone in claiming illustrious ancestors. In England the Feildings, Earls of Denbigh and Desmond, long boasted of their descent from the Counts of Habsburg-Laufenburg, a cadet branch of the Imperial House, until the late Dr. J. Horace Round shattered their equilibrium by proving that the claim was based on a seventeenth-century forgery. Oswald Barron relates in high good humor the story of a mid-nineteenth-century fabricated pedigree showing the descent of the Scottish family of Coulthart from a Roman soldier named "Coulthartus I," and how it ingloriously faded away after the antiquarian George Burnett focused his penetrating gaze on it, only to be resurrected subsequently by a genealogist who should have known better.

Some of the great European families who did not need spectacular ancestry because their achievements were spectacular enough nevertheless yearned for greater antiquity than the records provided. Adam Wandruszka, in his book *The House of Habsburg* (1964), reports that in the past there were attempts to trace that great imperial house (my "former ancestor") through Roman patrician families to Julius Caesar and through him to the Trojan hero Aeneas, who seems to have had a special fascination for our medieval forefathers. Duke Amadeus VIII of Savoy (later Pope Felix V) was not content to trace his descent from the eleventh century Umberto Biancamano (Humbert the White Handed); when he was elevated from the rank of count to that of a reigning duke he felt the need for greater genealogical glory. In his case we know who the forger was. Jean d'Orville alias Cabaret was hired to do the trick, and his "researches" took the duke's pedigree back to the dynasty of the Dukes of Saxony who produced the German King Henry the Fowler, and the Emperors Otto I, II, and III. Later writers made additions to this pedigree. It is said that down to the twentieth century the Italian rulers of the House of Savoy believed in this fanciful pedigree. (Robert Katz, *The Fall of the House of Savoy*, pp. 13-15.) The Fabian *gens* of ancient Rome seems to have had a fascination for European families. The princely House of Massimo once believed in its descent from the family of

Quintus Fabius Maximus Cunctator, the great enemy of Hannibal in the Second Punic War. Another legendary descendant of the Fabians was the German noble family of von Boyneburg. But it was left to the Hungarian princely House of Esterhazy to produce a pedigree that surpassed all others: "Adam Esterhazy, first of the name, Adam his son, second of the name, Adam his son, third of the name, under whom God created the world." (Georges Maurevert, "GENEALOGIES Fabuleuses," *Mercure de France*, 15 August 1921, p. 97.)

Here in America we not only claim kings but we ascend into the heavens to annex divine ancestors. In 1879 Albert Welles published a book in which he traced George Washington's ancestry to the Norse god Odin. We thought this claim had quietly disappeared when in 1956 another book came off the press with another family's descent from Odin. The Cadwaladers of Philadelphia really had the most splendid pedigree of all. Their pedigree, brought to America in 1683, showed that the family through a long series of Welsh worthies was sprung from the Greco-Roman gods Jupiter and Saturn, who in turn were derived from "Adam, the son of God," all in the direct male line! (Thomas Allen Glenn, *Welsh Founders of Pennsylvania*, i:32-35.)

A favorite royal ancestor of American families is Pharamond, purportedly a fifth-century king of the Franks. He, however, never existed. He was a creation of an eighth-century monk.

We have devoted considerable space to falsified royal lineages of American families. The fact is that quite a number of our early colonists had valid connections with English royalty. Such well-known seventeenth-century settlers as Gov. Thomas Dudley of Massachusetts; Col. George Reade of Virginia; Gov. Roger Ludlow of Connecticut; Anne Hutchinson, the religious liberal; Obadiah Bruen of Massachusetts; Elder William Wentworth of New Hampshire; Sarah Ludlow, wife of Col. John Carter of Virginia; George Elkington of New Jersey; Dr. Richard Palgrave of Massachusetts; John Barclay of New Jersey; Thomas Gordon of New Jersey; and many others have descents from noble and royal families. Their descendants are eligible for membership in such pre-colonial hereditary societies as the Order of the Crown in America, the Order of the Crown of Charlemagne in the United States of America, the National Society Daughters of the Barons of Runnemede, the Descendants of the Illegitimate Sons and Daughters of the Kings of Britain (popularly called the Royal Bastards), and the Baronial Order of Magna Charta (exclusively male; the other organizations admit both male and female members).

What are the bases for tracing royal and noble ancestry? For many years people regarded *Your Family Tree* by David Starr Jordan and Sarah Louise Kimball as Holy Writ. Dr. Jordan was a distinguished biologist and historian, but no genealogist. Neither was Miss Kimball!

Published in 1929, this book was seized upon eagerly by those seeking illustrious ancestors, not realizing that many of the descents are ridiculous, such as the ancestry of the Kings of Scythia and Ireland back to "Baoth, who received Scythis as his lot upon the division by Japhet, son of Noah." Charlemagne is proclaimed a descendant of Aeneas, the Trojan hero in Homer's *Iliad*, the line being taken through the Caesars and Pharamond (of course!) to the great emperor. Alfred the Great is traced through thirty-eight generations to "Noe" (the biblical Noah). The ancestry of kings, queens, presidents, statesmen, and many others is given. Among others, the pedigree of President Grant is known to be a forgery, and that of President Buchanan seems to be a lot of unidentified Buchanans strung together without dates, places, and wives. President Lincoln's "royal ancestry" is also suspect. Fortunately, *Your Family Tree* is not cited as often as it used to be, but regrettably it has been reprinted by the Genealogical Publishing Company, so it is again available for those who believe in fairy tales.

Charles H. Browning's *Americans of Royal Descent* (in several editions) and *Some "Colonial Dames" of Royal Descent*, published at the turn of this century, are also regarded as sacred writings by some people. Mr. Browning did not go into the flights of fancy that Jordan and Kimball enjoyed: he began his pedigrees with historic kings. But even so, he perpetuated a large number of errors. In the later editions he did try to correct the errors in the earlier ones, but even so, his work has to be treated with care. His one good scholarly work was *Welsh Settlement in Pennsylvania* (1912, reprinted by GPC, in 1969).

Another work to beware of is John S. Wurts's *Magna Charta* (8 vols., New York: Brookfield Publishing Company, 1942-54). While filled with glowing accounts of the Magna Charta Sureties and a proper veneration of the Great Charter as the basis for English and American law, the work also contains numerous errors and a silly pedigree showing Edward III as forty-fifth in descent from Boadicea, the heroic Queen of the Iceni who led an unsuccessful revolt against the Romans in the first Christian century. In one place he calls Boadicea (more properly, Boudicca) Victoria, which name she certainly never bore. Wurts should never be accepted as authoritative. It should not even be read.

In 1941 the Order of the Crown of Charlemagne in the United States of America published volume I of *Pedigrees of Some of the Emperor Charlemagne's Descendants*, compiled by Marcellus Donald R. von Redlich, LL.B., LL.D., Ph.D., with a Foreword by Professor Arthur Adams, Ph.D. This work was the best of its kind that had appeared up to that time. However, it is not free from error and one pedigree is chronologically impossible. Too much space is devoted to the descents from Charlemagne of the reigning families of Austria, Bavaria, Belgium, Great Britain, Italy, Netherlands, Norway, Saxony, Spain, the deposed

French House of Bourbon, and some of the princely families. It would have been wiser to have taken up these pages with lineages of American families. Wurts and Browning gave no sources for their data; neither did von Redlich, but he provided at the end of his book a bibliography of twelve and half pages.

The Order of the Crown of Charlemagne has continued the work begun by von Redlich. In 1974 it published volume II of *Pedigrees of Some of the Emperor Charlemagne's Descendants*, compiled by Aileen Lewers Langston and J. Orton Buck, Jr., with a foreword by the Genealogist General, Timothy Field Beard, who wrote, in eighty-five pages, a splendid dissertation on genealogical publications in all parts of the country. The Order published volume III of the *Pedigrees*, compiled by J. Orton Buck and Timothy Field Beard (1978). These two volumes contain the lineages of members of the Order. There are no citations to sources. Some of the pedigrees are known to be in error.

The Reverend Frederick Lewis Weis, an authority on the colonial clergy and author of six books on the subject, was also much interested in genealogy and especially the royal ancestry of New England colonists. In the 1950s he published two books, *Ancestral Roots of Sixty Colonists Who Came to New England between 1623 and 1650*, and *The Magna Charta Sureties, 1215, The Barons Named in the Magna Charta and Some of their Descendants Who Settled in America before 1650*. Dr. Arthur Adams consented to the use of his name on the title page, but Weis was the compiler.

These books are better than their predecessors, Wurts and Browning, and they have the advantage of citations to works consulted. Many of the pedigrees were sent to the compiler by friends whom he trusted. A large number of errors appeared in the books, and Dr. Weis, who died in 1966, did his best to correct them. Since then the Genealogical Publishing Company has brought out new editions under the editorship of Walter Lee Sheppard, Jr. He has corrected many of the pedigrees and eliminated generations that he found unsatisfactory. In one of his Prefaces he says: "Lastly, all genealogists and the general public are warned, that although I consider this the best book of its kind in print, it is NOT a reference work and should NOT be cited (any more than any other similar work) as evidence on a lineage blank for membership in a hereditary society. Go to the source material for this kind of thing. To the degree that sources are cited in this text, it will help you to find the proper reference." Unfortunately, many applicants for membership in pre-colonial hereditary societies fail to heed this warning, and cite only Weis and Sheppard. That is not true genealogical research. The applicant should buckle down and investigate all sources and references and cite them (as well as Weis and Sheppard) in his paper. We might note that *Ancestral Roots* has gone far beyond the sixty New England colonists of the original volume. Settlers in New York, New Jersey, Virginia, and other colonies, who came before and after Weis's cut-off date of 1650 are included. The name really should be changed in future editions to *Ancestral Roots of American Colonists*, or something of the sort.

So much for American books on royal ancestry. Among those published in Great Britain, mention may be made of G. E. Cokayne's *The Complete Peerage*, new edition (13 vols. in 14, 1910-59) and his *The Complete Baronetage* (5 vols. 1900-09). Sir James Balfour Paul's *The Scots Peerage* (9 vols., 1904-14) is excellent for Scottish noble families from whom many Americans descend. The researcher should also study the writings of such eminent genealogists as J. Horace Round and Oswald Barron, who exposed many of the fallacies in traditional British genealogy. William Farrer's *Honours and Knights' Fees* (3 vols., 1923-24) is an excellent study of medieval English pedigrees. Distinguished periodicals that should be searched include *The Ancestor*, *The Genealogist*, and *The Genealogist's Magazine*. Burke's *Peerage and Baronetage*, *Landed Gentry*, and *Dormant, Abeyant, Forfeited and Extinct Peerages* should not be used as authorities, only as providing clues for research.

The only way to try to find a descent from British and European nobility and royalty is to collect every bit of information about the immigrant ancestor to determine his home abroad. Not only should a researcher review such periodicals as *The New England Historical and Genealogical Register* and *The American Genealogist*, in which appear many articles dealing with overseas ancestry, but he should also search all family and public records to determine the ancestor's home before his immigration to America. The late Karl Friedrich von Frank used to lament that Americans simply did not do their homework before asking him to undertake researches on their behalf. It doesn't do any good to say, "My ancestor, Johann Jakob Schmidt, came to Pennsylvania in 1750; please send me his ancestry (by return mail?)." One woman wrote to me: "I understand you are an expert on German genealogy. Please tell me what office to write in Germany for my ancestry." (That was the complete letter; my reply was longer!) You must know the village, town, or city abroad where your ancestors lived; otherwise, research cannot be undertaken for you. It would be well for the researcher to read Dr. Adams's foreword to von Redlich's *Pedigrees of Some of the Emperor Charlemagne's Descendants*. He describes the procedures he followed to try to find a royal line. It was not easy, but by persistence and intelligence he succeeded in his quest. Sometimes the search is long and tedious, but if successful it is very rewarding.

Persons interested in tracing their ancestry to noble and royal families and who wish a splendid bibliography on the subject should read John Insley Coddington's chapter, "Royal and Noble Genealogy," in The American Society of Genealogists' textbook, *Genealogical Research: Methods and Sources* (revised edition, 1980), 1:402-22. He discusses briefly the development of research in this field and how it reached its present high standards. Especially important are his citations to the numerous works published in the British Isles and the continent of Europe—Germany, France, Italy, Switzerland, Austria, Belgium, the Netherlands, Luxembourg, Spain, Portugal, the Scandinavian countries, Finland, Russia, the Balkans, and the one-time Byzantine empire. Many of the works are in languages other than English, but all are worth examining for the data and clues they provide.

CHAPTER 10

THE COAT OF ARMS CRAZE

Many years ago Mrs. Florence Bridgers Culver, Herald of the National Genealogical Society, in a speech before the Society told the story of a woman named Howard who searched Burke's *General Armory* and finally found the insignia she liked. It was the armorial bearings of the Duke of Norfolk, Premier Duke and Premier Earl of England and head of the illustrious House of Howard. She had the arms engraved on her personal stationery and placed on the doors of her automobile. As Mrs. Culver remarked, "She was thus proclaiming that she was the Duke of Norfolk!"

Many people of English, Scottish, Welsh, and Irish ancestry look through Burke's *General Armory*, or, if they are of European descent, the two-volume Rietstap's *Armorial General*, and annex coats of arms to which they are not entitled. This practice has been encouraged by peddlers of coats of arms who, if they cannot find a genuine one to sell to prospective customers, will gladly provide a spurious coat of arms. This is the way Halbert's of Bath, Ohio, operated. They called their products "family name coats of arms." There is no such thing as a "family name coat of arms." Armorial bearings were granted to a certain individual, and only his descendants in the male line are entitled to them. Collateral branches of the same family may not bear them.

Halbert's and Sanson Institute of Heraldry at Boston are probably the two best-known firms that sell arms to gullible people who crave them as a sign of social prestige. If they can find a coat of arms of a customer's name in Burke or Rietstap, they illustrate the coat of arms

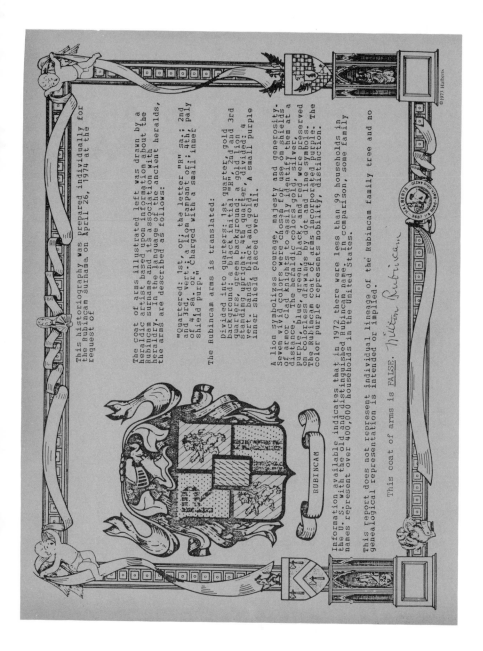

This historiography was prepared individually for the Rubincam surname on April 26, 1974 at the request of

The coat of arms illustrated left was drawn by a heraldic artist based upon information about the Rubincam surname and its association with heraldry, in the language of the ancient heralds, the arms are described as follows:

"Quartered: 1st, or; the letter "R" sa.; 2nd and 3rd, vert.; a lion rampant or; 4th, paly of 4, sa. or. Charged with a small inner shield purp."

The Rubincam arms is translated:

Divided into quarters: 1st quarter, gold background; a black initial "R". 2nd and 3rd quarters, green background; a gold lion on a standing upright. 4th quarter, divided: 4 vert. bands black and gold. A small purple inner shield placed over all.

A lion symbolizes courage, majesty and generosity. Several colors were close for use on shields. Several colors were close for use on shields. The heraldic colors identify them at a distance. The heraldic colors identify them at a distance. The heraldic colors were: red, green, blue, purple, black and silver. Reserved on colorless drawings by dot and line symbols. The Rubincam coat of arms incorporated purple. The color purple represents nobility, distinction.

Information available indicates that in 1972 there were less than 99 households in the U.S. with the old and distinguished Rubincam name. in comparison, some family names represent over 400,000 households in the United States.

This report does not represent individual lineage of the Rubincam family tree and no genealogical representation is intended or implied.

This coat of arms is FALSE. Milton Rubincam

RUBINCAM

False Rubincam Coat of Arms Invented By Halbert's of Bath, Ohio

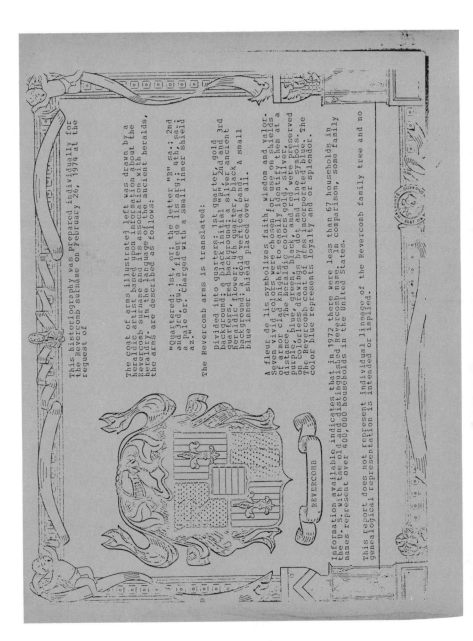

False Revercomb Coat of Arms Invented By Halbert's

according to the price the customer is prepared to pay, from a simple "report" and picture of the arms to a beautiful painting or an impressive plaque. If they are unable to find a genuine coat of arms for the customer's name, they manufacture one.

As an example, Halbert's wrote my oldest son, telling him that "the family name Rubincam has an exclusive and particularly beautiful Coat of Arms." He was going to throw the letter away when I induced him to send for the report—the $2.95 variety, of course. When it came the shield was divided into four quarters. In the first quarter was a large letter "R." This signified that the arms belonged to the Rubincam family—not Ross, not Robinson, not Rumford, but Rubincam. In the second and third quarters was a golden lion rampant. We were solemnly informed that the lion "symbolizes courage, majesty and generosity." In the fourth quarter were four vertical bands, black and gold. A small purple inner shield was placed over all. The report says, "The coat of arms illustrated left was drawn by a heraldic artist based upon the information about the Rubincam surname and its association with heraldry"— which "association" is nonexistent. The letter "R" in the first quarter is ridiculous. No coat of arms quartered has the initial letter of any surname. Incidentally, when a coat of arms is quartered it indicates that there are heiresses somewhere in the ancestral background. I'd love to know who my heiress ancestors were, according to the faked coat of arms!

A member of the Southern branch of my family (Revercomb) sent me a copy of the coat of arms purchased by her father from Halbert's. It, too, was quartered, with the inevitable "R" in the first quarter. In the second and third quarters we find a silver ancient heraldic flower (a fleur de lis). In the fourth quarter is a vertical band on a black background. A small blue inner shield is placed over all. Now, since the Rubincams and Revercombs are branches of the same family, they should have the same arms, with a difference, to distinguish members of one branch from their kinsmen of the other branch. We are told that this coat is also "based upon information about the Revercomb family with heraldry." In no instance, of course, does Halbert cite sources for any of its coats of arms.

I have a large file on Halbert's, since I was supplying information to a Post Office attorney twelve years ago when it was under investigation because of complaints and the unfavorable publicity it received. Among the exhibits I collected, one was from a friend named Carousso, who told me that the coat of arms he bought from Halbert's was not authentic. His name is not Italian but Greek—originally Karoussos. (Of course, a large "C" appeared in the first quarter!)

Sanson Institute of Heraldry also seems to manufacture arms for customers. When I was teaching a course in genealogy at the Catholic University of America one of my students showed me two coats of arms her father had purchased from Halbert's and Sanson. Of course, they were as different as the sun and moon. But Sanson did give a source: *Dizionario Storico Nobilare* (*sic*) *Italiano*. No such work exists. I searched the *Dizionario Storico-Blasonico delle Famiglie Nobili Estinte e Florente*, by Giovanni Battista di Crollalanza, and also Vittorio Spreti's *Enciclopedia Storico-Nobiliara Italiana*. The name I was seeking (Tontodonato) was not included among the Italian families entitled to coat armor.

I've been told that Halbert's has gone out of business but has started up again under another name. How true this is I don't know. Sometimes humorous stories about this firm have been published in the press. Its computers sometimes ran berserk. *The Tri-State Trader* for 12-17 August 1974 reported that the St. James Episcopal Church at Baton Rouge, Louisiana, received a letter addressed to Mr. Stjames E Ch, offering "a particularly and exclusive beautiful Coat of Arms for the name Ch." "This may surprise you," the computer said chattily, "since Ch is an extremely rare name. Of the 60 million households in the U.S. less than 99 are Ch households."

I have been going on at some length about the peddlers of arms for I want the reader to stay away from them. Please do not be beguiled by their sugar-sweet language about beautiful "family name coats of arms" and the association of one's family with heraldry.

There is another misuse of coats of arms: the publication of family histories or genealogies with beautiful coats of arms as the frontispiece. I have reviewed many books that cannot trace the families in question beyond the immigrant ancestor, yet the compilers look in Burke or Rietstap, find a coat of arms of a family bearing the same name, and promptly claim it. Very few compilers honestly say, "We cannot prove that we have a coat of arms, but the one portrayed here belongs to another family of our name." When compilers include in their books coats of arms to which they have no right they mislead present-day members of the family into believing they are entitled to the arms.

A very serious violation of the rules of heraldry occurred a couple of years ago when a history of the Griesemer family, which had come to Pennsylvania in 1730, was published. The family was of German origin, the name originally being Griesheimer. The compiler did a fine job documenting her family and making a judicious use of secondary materials. But she made one deplorable mistake—the adoption of a coat of arms to which her family was not entitled. She found in Rev. Ammon Stapleton's *Memorials of the Huguenots*, a very unsafe guide, a theory that the Griesemers were derived from the noble de Croismare family of Normandy. In the first chapter of her book she traced the history of the de Croismares from 1045 without establishing a connection, of course, with the Griesheimers. To make matters worse, she adopted the arms of the Marquis de Croismare, the head of his ancient house, and labelled them Griesemer. This is highly improper.

Many American families are indeed entitled to display coats of arms. The New England Historic Genealogical Society at Boston has a Committee on Heraldry which for many years has been investigating coats of arms claimed or used by Americans and has published a series of Rolls of Arms of United States families entitled to them.

The following quotation is taken from a paper entitled "Heraldry for United States Citizens," prepared years ago by the Board for Certification of Genealogists in response to complaints and questions about peddlers of coats of arms:

"If your male line immigrant ancestor from England was entitled to use a coat of arms, then you have the right under English law to use this same coat of arms. If he had no such right, then neither do you [unless you buy a grant of arms for yourself from the College of Arms]. Thus, to establish the right under English (or German, French, Swiss, etc.) law to a coat of arms, it is necessary to prove your uninterrupted male line descent from someone who was legally entitled to use this coat armor. No 'heraldry institute' or 'heraldic artist' can look up a surname and provide the correct arms for you without first proving your descent. If they say they can do so, then they are guilty of fraud."

CHAPTER 11

FRAUDULENT
PEDIGREES

A ll through history frauds and forgeries have been perpetrated on un-suspecting people, even on whole nations. One of the most famous was the Donatio Constantini (Donation of Constantine), which allegedly was a grant by Emperor Constantine the Great to Pope Silvester I (314-335) and his successors of spiritual supremacy over all matters of faith and worship, and of temporal dominion over Rome, Italy, and the entire western world. The only problem is, no one had ever heard of it until the monks of St. Denis, near Paris, concocted it shortly before the year 800. And so it has gone on through the centuries. Newspaper readers will recall that only a few years ago a certain Konrad Kujau forged the so-called "Hitler diaries" with such skill that they are acclaimed as genuine by an eminent English scholar and three well-known publications—all of whom were forced to admit shamefacedly that they had been duped and had mislead the world. The motives for creating forgeries are chiefly vanity and greed.

So it is with genealogy. We have already mentioned some of the more outstanding forgeries—the Feildings's boast of descent from the House of Habsburg, the fictitious origin of the Dukes of Bedford, the falsified origin of the House of Savoy, and the fabricated pedigree of the Scottish Coultharts. The other faked pedigrees we mentioned were based on wishful thinking and ignorance, not deliberate forgeries. The reader who is interested in pursuing the subject of British genealogical frauds should read some of the articles in *The Ancestor*, beginning with vol. 1 in 1902.

Here in America we have not been free from this vice. The first American professional genealogist was Horatio Gates Somerby, who was born at Newburyport, Massachusetts, 24 December 1805. After a brief career as an artist he removed to London after 1845, and specialized in working out the English origins of New England families. He was a member of the New England Historic Genealogical Society and the Massachusetts Historical Society (which has a large number of his unpublished manuscripts). He was an expert on English genealogical sources and successfully made the connection between many families in America and their English ancestors. However, if he could not prove a line of descent for a family he arranged to give them a plausible pedigree. Some of these may be correct, but need strengthening. The pedigree he prepared for the Gould family, as an example, Walter Goodwin Davis says "is, in all probability sound, but the Goulds were prolific and, in my opinion, further research, which I am not prepared to make, might strengthen it." (*The Ancestry of Dudley Wildes, 1759-1820*, p. 101.) Persons descended from families on which Somerby worked should examine their pedigrees with the greatest care to determine their accuracy or lack thereof.

We have already made the acquaintance of Dr. George Gains Brewster, who did not know of the 1752 calendar change and so left a baby out of the family records because he thought the child was illegitimate. Mr. Davis gives us further information of him in *The Ancestry of Joseph Waterhouse, 1754-1837*, pp. 64-68. The good doctor was determined to be descended from Elder William Brewster of the *Mayflower*, and when he could not make the connection he drew up seventeenth-century documents in his nineteenth-century handwriting and, what was worse, altered public records, again in his modern script. In one case the original name was erased by scratching clear through the leaf so that the name of one of the early Brewsters is written partly on the following leaf. Dr. Brewster was unmasked in his own lifetime by Judge James Savage, the compiler of the celebrated dictionary of New England settlers, and he died discredited in 1872, by coincidence the same year that saw Somerby's demise. In Dr. Brewster's case, the frauds were not for financial gain but to please his vanity and a yearning to be counted among Elder Brewster's posterity.

In the first part of this century Gustave Anjou operated. He was an expert on New York records and published two volumes of Ulster County wills. He did research professionally and pleased many clients by establishing connections with British ancestors. One family he worked on was that of John Ogden, who settled in Southampton, Long Island, in 1640. The English pedigree, going back to 1453, was published in William Ogden Wheeler's *The Ogden Family in America, Elizabethtown Branch, and Their English Ancestry; John Ogden, the Pilgrim, and His*

Descendants, 1640-1906 (1907). Mr. Wheeler says that to identify the pioneer's home in England had been a perplexing problem, but "There seems no room for doubt, however, that John Ogden, the Pilgrim...came from Bradley Plain, in Co. Southants, and that several generations of his forefathers had lived there before him." Mr. Wheeler said that the pedigree was confirmed by a genealogist "who claims personal knowledge of the church records at Bradley Plain, Hampshire, and of several other English records and authorities." The genealogist was identified in a footnote: "Gustave Anjou, 116 Nassau St., New York."

As my wife is descended from John Ogden, who in time became deputy governor of the Province of East New Jersey, I was delighted when I first saw the pedigree a half century ago, and tried to confirm it. I was unsuccessful, and finally wrote to Charles Carroll Gardner, then one of the foremost authorities on New Jersey families. He replied that there was no proof for the pre-American genealogy printed in the Ogden book. As a matter of fact, the parish of Bradley Plain does not exist, in Hampshire or anywhere else.

Anjou was also commissioned to trace the ancestry of Richard Higgins, who settled at Plymouth about 1632. He identified the immigrant with Richard Higgins, born 1 August 1603, and traced him to Rev. John Higgins, who was instituted Rector of Blatchley in Newport Hundred, Bucks County, in 1561. This pedigree was accepted by Orra Eugene Monnette and published in *The New York Genealogical and Biographical Record*, vols. 46 and 47. Mrs. Katherine Chapin Higgins, in her splendid and well-documented genealogy of her husband's family, *Richard Higgins, A Resident and Pioneer Settler at Plymouth and Eastham, Massachusetts, and at Piscataway, New Jersey* (1918), pp. 17-18, analyzed the evidence and determined that there was no proof that the American Richard was the boy born in 1603.

In my files is a pedigree, forwarded to me by a lady in Falls Church, Virginia, entitled *The Maxwell Family of Scotland, Ireland, and the United States of America*. On the title page appears the following: "Gustave Anjou, Ph.D., the Genealogist, states as follows:

"Your line is, of course, indicated in red, and I have given 13 connected generations previous to your own; I have little reason to doubt, however, that the generations as given on pages 1-15, are of your line, but I do not want to make a definite assertion to that effect."

This is, of course, a warning not to accept the lineage. The American immigrant, Hugh Maxwell, born *ca.* 1701, is said to have come from Ireland to America in 1733. Without any evidence whatever, Anjou made Hugh a son of Samuel Maxwell, and traced the ancestry to the Maxwells of Kirkconnell, a branch of the historic House of Maxwell. The line is traced to Herbert Maxwell of Kirkconnell, who died in 1637, and his younger son, Robert. Robert is said to have married Margaret

Abernethy and in time to have become progenitor of the American family. A pedigree of the Maxwells of Kirkconnell appears in William Fraser's *The Book of Carlaverock; Maxwells, Earls of Nithsdale, Lords Maxwells and Herries* (1873), 1:600-601. Herbert Maxwell of Kirkconnell is shown to have had, besides two daughters and an illegitimate son, four sons, of whom the fourth was Robert. But, no further data is given about Robert—no dates, no wife, no children. Hence, this pedigree collapses at once. In the Anjou pedigrees that I have seen, he gives no clues that point to the main stock in the British Isles. He offers no reasons for assigning the American families to the lines he claims. He died in 1942, after making and losing a fortune selling pedigrees at prices ranging from $250 to $9000.

A rather elaborate fabrication of genealogical data concerning the Foulke family of Dorchester County, Maryland, was worked out by Miss Leslie A. Ricardo, a genealogist, in the early 1970s. The evidence came to light after her death. Involved were notarized copies of "records" signed by John Berry, custodian of the Tuckahoe Burial Records (who could not be found afterward); the Tuckahoe Burial Books (Quaker records, which also could not be found and apparently were the figment of Miss Ricardo's fertile imagination); a claim that the "Burial Books" were picked up and taken to Salt Lake City for reproduction by two representatives of the Genealogical Society of The Church of Jesus Christ of Latter-day Saints (the Society had no knowledge of the books or of the two men who were allegedly its employees), and a forged signature, etc. A thorough investigation of Miss Ricardo's work was undertaken by Roy A. Foulke, in cooperation with the Friends Historical Library at Swarthmore College, Swarthmore, Pennsylvania, the Maryland Hall of Records at Annapolis, authorities on Quaker records, and local officials. Mr. Foulke tells the story in detail in his *Foulke Family*, second edition, revised and updated (1974).

Fortunately, cases such as those related above are rare. Most professional genealogists are completely honest, base their work on record evidence, and report to their clients their findings. The high standards of the business are maintained by the Board for Certification of Genealogists and the Association of Professional Genealogists.

CHAPTER 12

THE STUDY OF HISTORY

One of the requirements of a good genealogist is a knowledge of history. He must know about the changing of state and county lines. A family may have lived a generation in the same house on the same land and not moved an inch, yet in thirty years may have resided in three counties and two states. The genealogist must know about migration patterns and the trails over which his ancestors moved westward or southward. He must know the ethnic groups that settled in the area of his research, about laws governing probate, immigration and naturalization, and so on.

Our history can be confusing. Richard S. Lackey, in his chapter on Mississippi in *Genealogical Research: Methods and Sources*, 2:189 (revised edition, 1983), wrote: "If the genealogist forgets that the coastal area of the Mississippi Territory was a part of British West Florida and later of Spanish West Florida until after the War of 1812, research problems may arise. It is quite possible to find a record of a person born prior to 1812 indicating Florida or West Florida as a place of birth when, in fact, one of the coastal counties of Mississippi or Alabama may have been the place of birth."

Prior to the Revolutionary War, parts of Pennsylvania were claimed by three other colonies because of contradictory charters granted by our kings to the founders. Connecticut claimed the upper third of Pennsylvania and over into Ohio. In the middle of the eighteenth century, two companies threw Connecticut settlers into the northeastern area of Pennsylvania, comprising the present counties of Luzerne, Wyoming, Columbus, Bradford, Lycoming, Montour, Susquehanna, Lackawanna, Pike, and Monroe. If you have an ancestor in that area and don't know where to go next, try the Connecticut State Library at Hartford, for your ancestor may have been among those who, in the 1750s, made the trek westward from Connecticut to Pennsylvania. Also, your ancestor(s) may be mentioned in the excellent eleven-volume work *The Susquehanna Company Papers.* (The papers of the other colonizing group, the Delaware Company, seem to have been destroyed.) Maryland claimed the lower fringe of Pennsylvania counties, from a point above Philadelphia. Families who lived in Chester County, Pennsylvania, in 1763 may have found themselves in Cecil County Maryland, after Mason and Dixon had completed their great survey in 1767. Virginia claimed the southwestern counties of Fayette, Westmoreland, Washington, and parts of Allegheny and Beaver counties, and created them (with certain counties now in West Virginia) into the District of West Augusta and attached it to Augusta County. Your ancestors in that part of Pennsylvania may have come from Virginia, and are recorded in Boyd Crumrine's *Virginia Court Records in Southwestern Pennsylvania...1775-1780.* (See chapter on Pennsylvania in *Genealogical Research: Methods and Sources,* 1:244-46, revised edition, 1980.) These claims were not settled until after the Revolutionary War. A good account of these problems is in *Pennsylvania Boundaries,* by William A. Russ, Jr. (Harrisburg: Pennsylvania Historical and Museum Commission; Pennsylvania History Studies No. 8, 1966).

Other states had similar problems. If William Penn had obtained all the land described in his charter, Pennsylvania would have extended to above Buffalo, New York. The Vermont area was claimed at various times by New York, New Hampshire, and Massachusetts. The genealogist working on families in disputed areas must be familiar with the history of the time and know where to look for records. Researchers of the so-called "burned counties" of Virginia must examine the records of adjoining counties in the hope of filling in the gaps caused by lost records. Families often owned properties in several states. As an example, Philadelphia families possessed lands in New Jersey, Delaware, and Maryland, and so the researcher must examine documents in all of those states if he is to make his genealogy reasonably complete.

It is important for the genealogist to know what trails his forefathers used to go from their original place of abode to distant regions. An excellent account by Marcus W. Lewis is *The Development of Early Emigrant Trails in the United States East of the Mississippi River* (NGS Special Publication No. 3, originally published in 1933 but reprinted in 1972 and at other times). The map accompanying this paper includes fifty-four principal trails. Two articles by John Insley Coddington deserve wider distribution than the Indiana Historical Society was able to give them. They are: "Patterns of Migration in the Colonial Period" (*The Hoosier Genealogist,* 9:1-6, January-February 1969), and "Patterns of Post Revolutionary Migration" (Ibid., 9:13-17, March-April 1969, published by the Genealogical Section of the Indiana Historical Society). He discusses the emigration of our ancestors from the British Isles and Europe, the various settlements and ethnic groups in the colonies, the migrations westward, the nineteenth and twentieth century emigrations from abroad, the economic, religious and other causes of the population movements, and so on.

Compilers of genealogists often introduce historical matter in their books without first checking for accuracy. Two ladies who wrote a very indifferent genealogy of the Gleim family of Pennsylvania said that the immigrant ancestors "sailed in 1754 from Wuertemberg (*sic*), Germany"—which is a pretty good trick when you consider that Wuerttemberg is entirely surrounded by land! They said that a ship, the *Minerva*, sailed from Rotterdam, 25 October 1748. Actually it arrived in Philadelphia on that date. I remember reviewing a book in which it was stated that progenitor "came from Prussia which is now called Germany." Prussia was never "called Germany"; it was a state (by the nineteenth century the largest state) in Germany.

It is distressing when the author of a book makes so many errors that one's confidence is shaken in him. George Leland Summer published *Newberry County, South Carolina: Historical and Genealogical* in 1950. The historical part is fairly good but the genealogical section is based on family traditions and hearsay not subjected to a critical examination. Summer made historical blunders that could have been avoided had he taken the trouble to read articles in *The Encyclopaedia Britannica* and any good history book. Examples: "During the latter part of the fourteenth and early fifteenth centuries the French Huguenots were expelled from their native land by the revocation of the Nantes" (*sic*). The fact is, the Huguenots did not exist in the fourteenth and fifteenth centuries (not until the sixteenth), and the Edict of Nantes was not revoked until 1685. "It so happened," we are informed in another place, "that the Queen of England was Charlotte Mecklenburg, daughter of the German Emperor." This would have been a great surprise to George III's queen, since "it so happened" that her father was the Duke of Mecklenburg-Strelitz, not the German (i.e. Holy Roman) Emperor. Again, we are told that William III of England was harassed by the Prince of Orange. That may be, but King William III was the Prince of Orange! We are also assured that the Scotch-Irish "felt the grossness of King William II of England" who lived some six centuries before the Scotch-Irish came into existence.

Another historical pitfall is the claim that an ancestor came from Prussia because the 1850, 1860, 1870, or 1880 censuses gave that as his home in Europe. Prussia was originally a small state in the northeastern part of Germany as that country was before the two World Wars. After being ruled successively by the Teutonic Knights and Poland, it came into possession of the House of Hohenzollern, who erected it into a duchy. Later on, when the Electors of Brandenburg took the title Kings in (afterwards of) Prussia (1701), all of the territories ruled by this aggressive family were called Prussia. By war, conquest, and inheritance their dominions spread across Germany to the Rhine. The *Encyclopedia of German-American Genealogical Research*, by Clifford Neal Smith and his wife, Anna Piszczan-Czaja Smith (New York & London: R. R. Bowker Company, 1978), p. 132, shows that by 1853 Prussia governed forty-eight territories that had formerly been independent or semi-independent. So if a man enumerated in one of the foregoing censuses said he was born in Prussia, it was Prussia at the time of the census but not necessarily so at the time of his birth. There were additional lands seized after 1853. For instance, Prussia went to war with Austria in 1866, and as a result it acquired the electorate of Hessen (-Kassel), the duchy of Nassau, and the Free City of Frankfurt. These were incorporated into the Prussian Province of Hessen-Nassau, and the inhabitants ceased to be Hessians, Nassauers, and Frankfurters but became Prussians. So to find the ancestor one must go not to the archives of old Prussia but to the archives of the former Hessian, Nassavian, and Frankfurter territories. In this century the present State of Hessen includes not only the areas mentioned above but the former grand duchy of Hessen (-Darmstadt) and the principality of Waldeck. To accomplish effective research in Germany one must study the makeup of the Holy Roman Empire (the Smiths' *Encyclopedia* lists between 300 and 400 states of the *Altreich* on pp. 114-43, with brief accounts of each). If the genealogist can identify the ancestral state in Germany, he must study the history of that territory to determine where his research must begin.

History and genealogy are so intertwined that one cannot do without the other.

CHAPTER 13

REVIEWING THE PERIODICAL LITERATURE

Since the first publication in 1847 of *The New England Historical and Genealogical Register* (our oldest genealogical periodical—indeed, as Timothy Field Beard reminds us in *How to Trace Your Family Roots* (1977), p. 57, the oldest in the world), magazines devoted to genealogical subjects have grown steadily in number. In the latter half of this century they have proliferated to an extraordinary degree. Many of them are published by genealogical societies, but a large number are published independently, such as *The American Genealogist*, *The Virginia Genealogist*, *The Kentucky Genealogist*, *The Georgia Genealogist*, *The Maryland and Delaware Genealogist*, *The Genealogist*, *Swedish-American Genealogist*, *Canadian Genealogist*, *French-Canadian and Acadian Genealogical Review*, *Lost in Canada?*, and *Mennonite Family History*. Mary K. Meyer's *Directory of Genealogical Societies in the USA and Canada* (4th edition, 1982) lists about 1,350 genealogical societies (national, state, provincial, county, local), most of which publish magazines, and 142 independent periodicals. These magazines cover a variety of subjects: family genealogies, ancestor tables, source materials (wills, deeds, tax lists, vital statistics, church registers, etc.), archival resources, book reviews, queries, evaluation of evidence, methods of research in America, foreign research, and so on. For researchers with overseas interests there are a large number of British and European periodicals: *The Genealogists' Magazine* (England), *The Scottish Genealogist* (Scotland), *Genealogie* (Germany), *Giornale araldico, storical, genealogico* (Italy), *Gens nostra, ons geslacht* (Netherlands), and many others.

Researchers interested in certain areas would be well advised to join genealogical societies in these areas in order to receive the magazines published by such societies. A wealth of information is contained in them. Libraries and historical and genealogical societies often display current issues of periodicals on racks or shelves so researchers may look them over for any items of interest.

But it would be well to browse through the bound back issues of magazines. Do not confine yourselves only to the periodicals of your areas. Browse in periodicals published far from your area of research, for sometimes one is in for a surprise. For instance, the 1919 volume of *The New England Historical and Genealogical Register* carries four installments of an article on marriage licenses of Prince George's County, Maryland, covering the period 1777-1824. Prince George's County is a small entity in Maryland and one would scarcely expect to find it so prominently displayed in a New England magazine. Recently, I was browsing through back issues of the *Bulletin* of the Seattle (Washington) Genealogical Society when I found in volumes 12-13 published in the 1960s baptisms and marriages from 1785 of the Congregational Church of Deer Island, Maine. A periodical published in the state of Washington is the least likely place one would expect to see Maine records!

Errors published in genealogies and family histories are usually corrected in periodicals. As an example, the Reverend Frederick Lewis Weis, in *One Thousand New England Ancestors of Frank Chester Harrington and Leora (Leighton) Harrington* (1958), stated (p. 181) that Miles Nutt (1598?-1671), of Malden, Massachusetts, married Sybil Tincknell (whom he erroneously called Tuicknell); he asserted that she was the mother of his only known daughter Sarah. This brought a reply from John Insley Coddington in *TAG*, 38:64 (January 1962): "Had the author bothered to check the periodical literature, he would have seen in this magazine, *supra*, vol. 31, pp. 90-101, an article by the present writer entitled 'Sybil Tincknell (Bibble) (Nutt) Doolittle and her Family,' which clearly shows, pp. 91-93, that Miles Nutt had no issue by Sybil, who was his second wife, and that Sarah was the offspring of Miles Nutt's first wife, whose name is unknown." Persons reading the Harrington book are misled into believing they are descended from Sybil Tincknell, whose ancestry goes back to the mid-sixteenth century.

In *TAG*, 53:78-78 (April 1977) Dr. Neil D. Thompson published an article entitled "The Douglass Family of Charles County, Maryland: Some Further Observations." He criticized a book on the same family by Harry Wright Newman, a well-known Maryland genealogist, pointing out errors and assumptions on the latter's part. Mr. Newman did much good work as an expert on Maryland records, but he was also prone to attach families to illustrious ancestors from whom they were not descended. The final paragraph reads: "Finally, it ought to be noted that I cited certain evidence [in a previous article on the Douglasses] for the possibility that the emigrant was son of Sir Robert Douglas of Blaikerston and had a lengthy ancestry, including royal descent. On the same evidence, adding nothing at all, Mr. Newman has asserted this connection as fact. It may be correct or it may not be. But genealogy has suffered so much already from speculation and wishful thinking on the subject of royal and noble ancestry for colonial immigrants that it seems a pity to publish yet another example of such pedigree-mongering. (On this point, the only proper verdict is the useful Scots 'not proven'; further work in the Scottish records is called for.") We should add Mr. Newman's name to Somerby's and Anjou's. If the reader is descended from a family whose British ancestry has been traced by him, the lines should be tested very carefully before being accepted. He was thoroughly familiar with records, and may indeed have made the connection. On the other hand, a lady once commissioned me to investigate the Scottish origin of her Maryland ancestor which he had compiled to admit her cousin to a pre-colonial society. The pedigree proved to be false.

The researcher should also study the book reviews, for here errors are often picked up and corrected. The periodicals that publish the most critical reviews are the *National Genealogical Society Quarterly*, *The American Genealogist*, *The New England Historical and Genealogical Register*, *The New York Genealogical and Biographical Record*, *Genealogical Journal* (organ of the Utah Genealogical Association, Salt Lake City), and *The Genealogist* (Neil D. Thompson, editor).

CHAPTER 14

CASE HISTORIES: A SELECTED BIBLIOGRAPHY

In the course of this text we have mentioned a number of articles dealing with pitfalls and how to combat them. The following bibliography of case histories is one which I provide as a handout for my lectures on "Pitfalls in Genealogical Research" and "Evaluation of Evidence." The titles mentioned in the text are repeated in the following list. Some other recommended works are: Richard S. Lackey, *Cite Your Sources: A Manual for Documenting Family Histories and Genealogical Records* (New Orleans: Polyanthos, Inc., 1980); Elizabeth Shown Mills and Dr. Gary B. Mills, "How to Properly Document Your Research Notes," *The Genealogical Helper*, 33:5, September-October 1979; Thomas H. Roderick, "Estimation of the Percentage of Genetically False Pedigrees," *TAG*, 37:4, October 1961; Eugene S. Stratton, C.G., "The Validity of Genealogical Evidence," *NGSQ*, 72:4, December 1984. The case histories presented below have been carefully selected as being among the best examples of how to assemble the evidence, evaluate it, and avoid the pitfalls.

Case Histories

1. Anderson, Robert Charles, "David Gay (*ca.* 1739-1815), of Onslow, Nova Scotia, and Lincolnville, Maine," *NGSQ*, 67:2, June 1979.

2. Barclay, Mrs. John E., "Five Jonathan Dunhams Untangled," *TAG*, 44:4, October 1968.

3. Cocke, Virginia Webb, "Mistaken Identity;" also, "My Grandson William Fleming Cocke," both in *The Virginia Genealogist*, 15:3, July-August 1975.

4. Coddington, John Insley, "Bigod," in Arthur Adams and Frederick Lewis Weis, *Magna Charta Sureties, 1215* (Baltimore: Genealogical Publishing Company, 3rd edition, 1979, edited by Walter Lee Sheppard, Jr.).

5. Jacobus, Donald Lines, *Genealogy as Pastime and Profession* (Baltimore: GPC, 2nd edition, 1968). Chapter XIII: "Case Histories."

6. McCracken, George E., "Too Many Jonathan Gilletts in Windsor," *TAG*, 56:2, April 1980.

7. Michaels, Brian E., "The Tree from the Stone. A Genealogical Puzzle Solved," *The Putnam County Genealogical Society Quarterly* (Florida) No. 3, Fall 1983. (A very difficult problem solved eventually by an Irish Catholic priest who knew Gaelic. Worth reading for the intricate steps taken to read a tombstone inscription.)

8. Mills, Elizabeth Shown, and Mills, Gary B., "The Genealogist's Assessment of Alex Haley's *Roots*," *NGSQ*, 72:1, March 1984.

9. Moriarty, G. Andrews, "The Origin of the Crowninshields," *TAG*, 25:4, October 1949.

10. Moriarty, G. Andrews, "Genealogical Problems," *NGSQ*, 50:3, September 1962. (Six New England and two medieval case histories.)

11. Pitman, H. Minot, "Genealogical Proof, Example: Hannah (Knapp) Weed," *TAG*, 37:4, October 1961.

12. Pitman, H. Minot, "Job 'Whipple' of Providence, Rhode Island," *TAG* 44:3, July 1968.

13. Rubincam, Milton, "The Identity and Ancestry of Sarah, Wife of Henry Parry of Pittsburgh, Pennsylvania," *NGSQ*, vol. 53, September 1965.

14. Rubincam, Milton, *Evidence: An Exemplary Study. A Craig Family Case History* (Washington, D.C.: National Genealogical Society, Special Publication No. 49, 1981).

15. Scott, Kenneth, "The Pretended Will of Colonel Joachim Staats of Albany, 1711," *NGSQ*, 63:2, June 1975.

16. Thompson, Neil D., "The Douglass Family of Charles County, Maryland. Some Further Observations," *TAG* 53:2, April 1977.

17. Zabriskie, George Olin, *Climbing Our Family Tree Systematically* (Salt Lake City: Parliament Press, 1969). Case histories.